| DATE DUE | | | Metro Litho
Oak Forest, IL 60452 |
|---|---|---|---|
| NOV 1 1 1993 | | | |
| FEB. 02 1995 | | | |
| JAN. 22 1996 | | | |
| OCT 15 | | | |
| DEC. 0 1996 | | | |
| OCT. 14 1997 | | | |
| FEB. 23 1998 | | | |
| JUN. 16 1998 | | | |
| | | | |
| | | | |
| | | | |

03354-9

289.3
JON

Jones, Helen Hinckley
Over the Mormon trail

DISCARDED

FOREWORD

"Frontiers of America" dramatizes some of the explorations and discoveries of real pioneers in simple, uncluttered text. America's spirit of adventure is seen in these early people who faced dangers and hardship blazing trails, pioneering new water routes, becoming Western heroes as well as legends, and building log forts and houses as they settled in the wilderness.

Although today's explorers and adventurers face different frontiers, the drive and spirit of these early pioneers in America's past still serve as an inspiration.

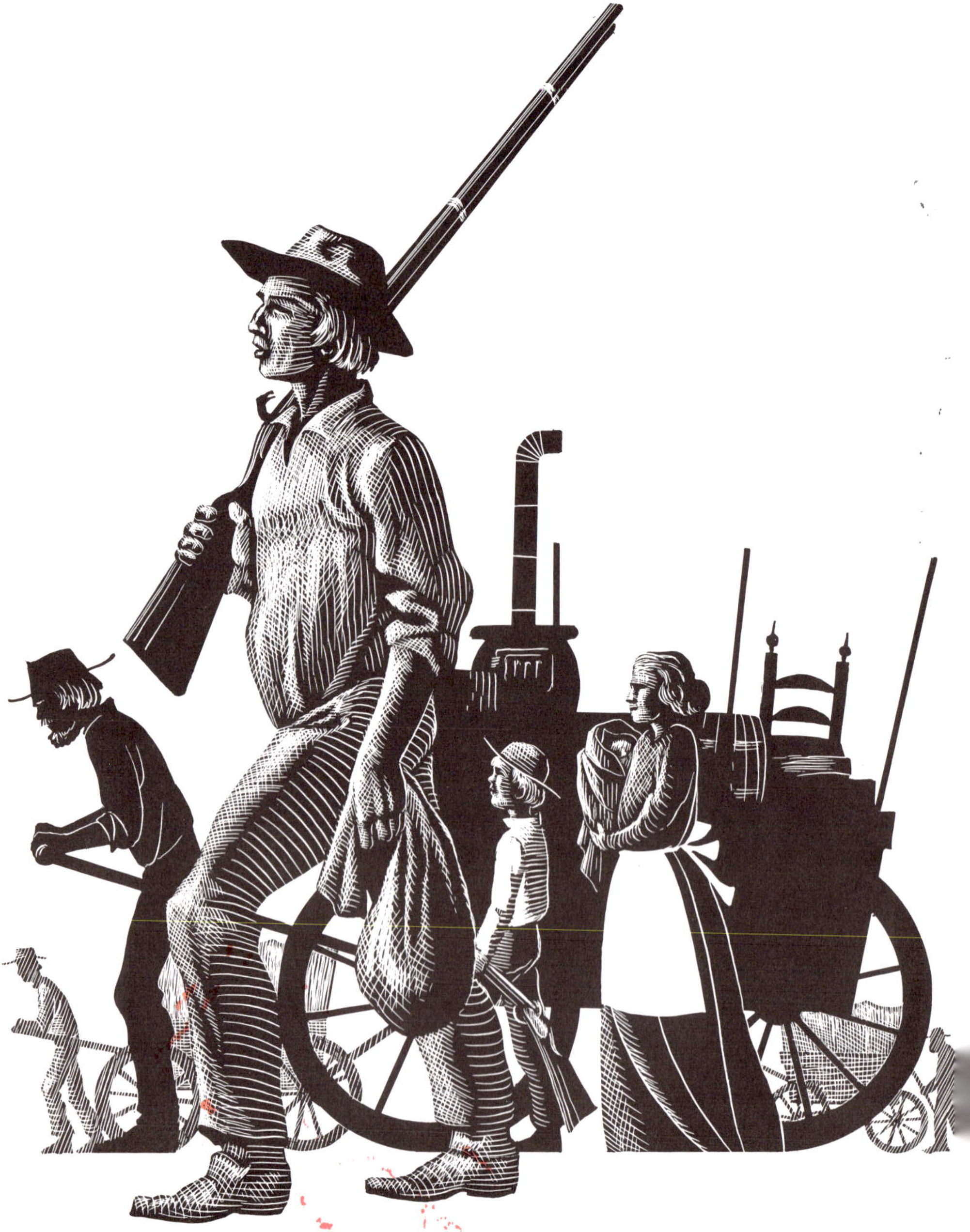

Frontiers of America

Over the
MORMON TRAIL

By Helen Hinckley Jones
Illustrations by Carol Rogers

CHILDRENS PRESS, CHICAGO

Library of Congress Cataloging in
Publication Data
Jones, Helen Hinckley, [date]
  Over the Mormon Trail.
  1. Mormons and Mormonism—Juvenile
fiction.   I. Title.
PZ7.J717.Ov   63-9706
ISBN 0-516-03354-9

Cover photograph courtesy
of the National Archives

New 1980 Edition
Copyright© 1960 by Regensteiner
Publishing Enterprises, Inc.
All rights reserved. Published
simultaneously in Canada.
Printed in the United States of America.
4 5 6 7 8 9 10 11 R 93 92 91 90

CONTENTS

NAUVOO, THE BEAUTIFUL, 9

THE GOOD SHIP *BROOKLYN*, 15

TWENTY THOUSAND PEOPLE MOVE, 26

HUNGRY, FOOTSORE BATTALION, 37

VALLEY OF THE GREAT SALT LAKE, 52

MILLIONS OF CRICKETS, 68

HANDCART PIONEERS, 75

THE IRON HORSE, 93

THE MORMON TRAIL GOES ON, 108

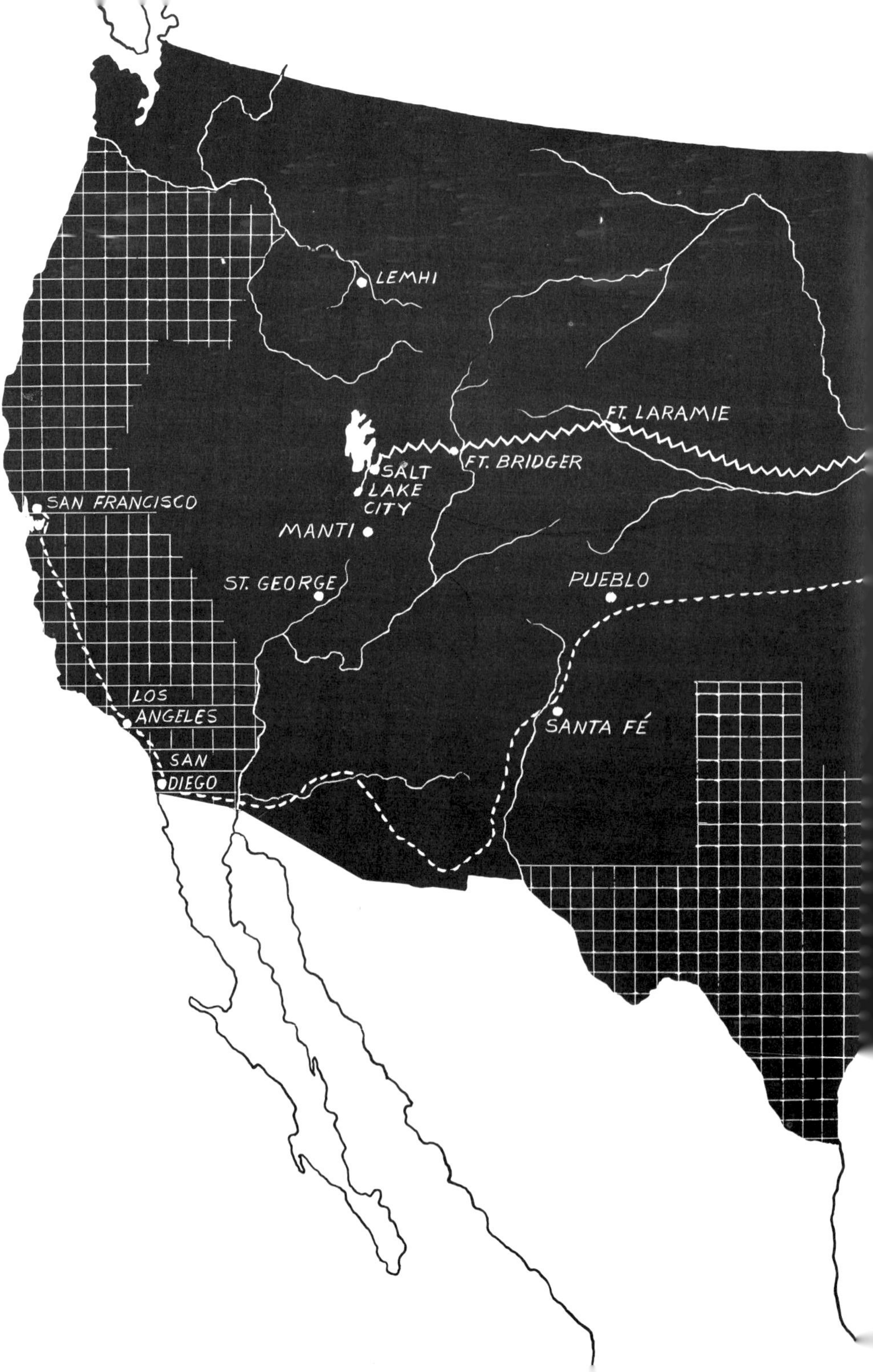
LEMHI
FT. LARAMIE
FT. BRIDGER
SALT LAKE CITY
SAN FRANCISCO
MANTI
ST. GEORGE
PUEBLO
SANTA FÉ
LOS ANGELES
SAN DIEGO

NEW YORK

WINTER QUARTERS
NAUVOO
FT. LEAVENWORTH

MORMON TRAILS

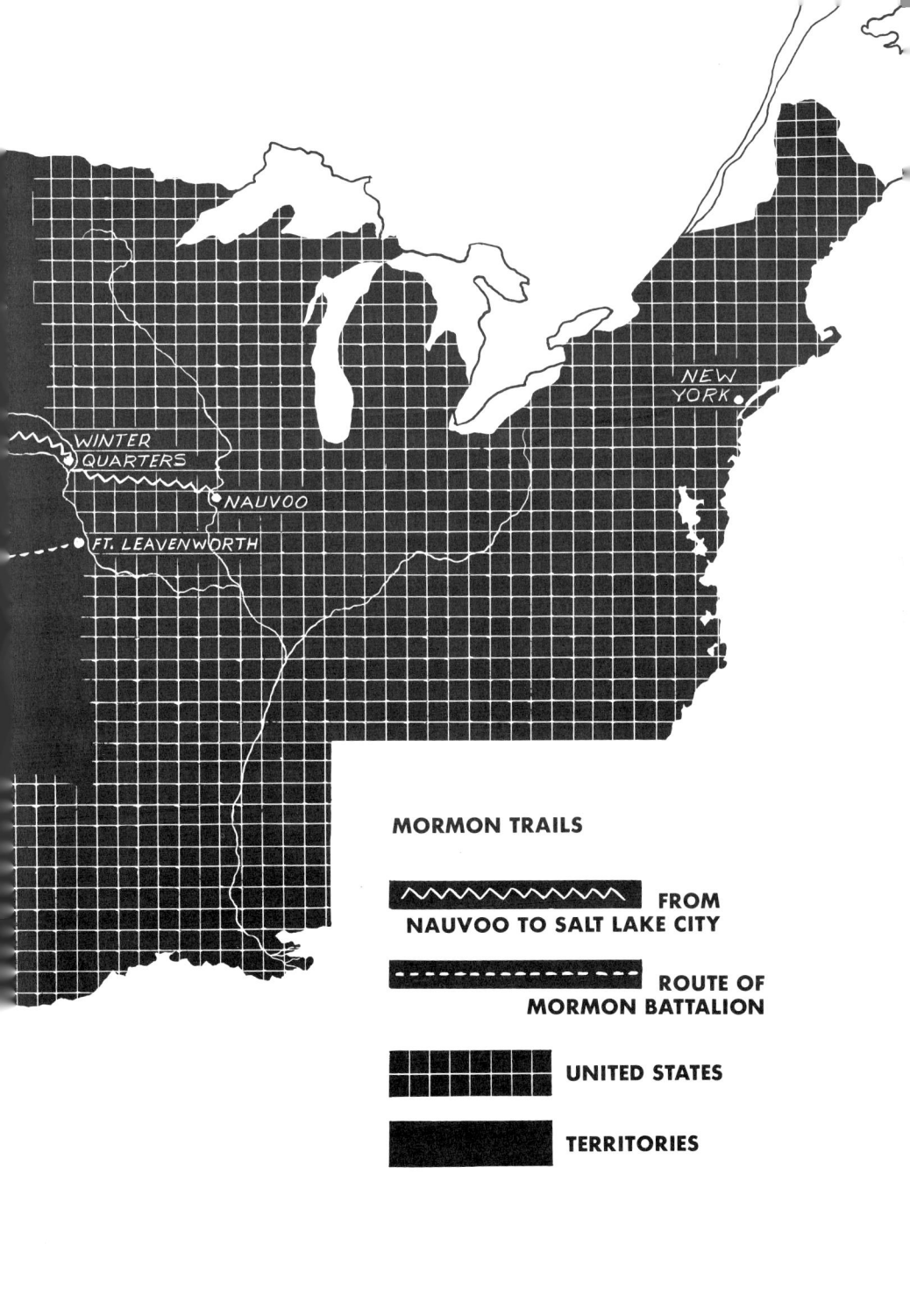

〜〜〜〜〜〜 **FROM NAUVOO TO SALT LAKE CITY**

------- **ROUTE OF MORMON BATTALION**

▦ **UNITED STATES**

▮ **TERRITORIES**

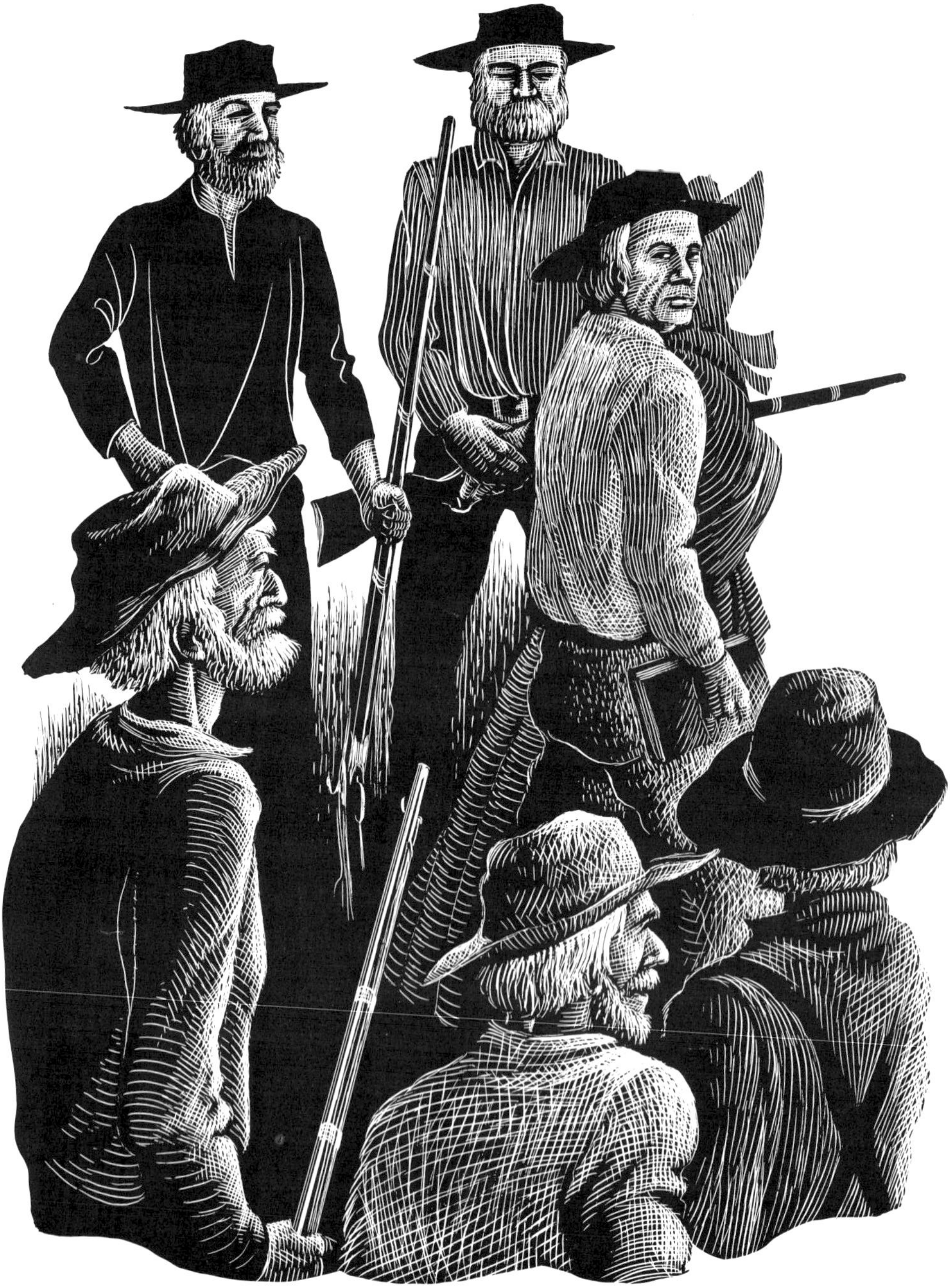

NAUVOO, THE BEAUTIFUL

In 1845 Nauvoo, surrounded on three sides by the Mississippi River, was the largest town in Illinois. St. Louis was the largest city on the frontier but Nauvoo was next in size. And Nauvoo was much more beautiful than St. Louis.

It was not a frontier village, not a sleepy river town, but a beautiful, busy city where 25,000 people lived and worked. There were grand two-story red brick houses with neat picket fences and carefully tended gardens and orchards. There was a steam sawmill, a flour mill, a tool factory, a foundry, and hundreds of shops and small factories. Skilled workmen from the British Isles and from New England worked in these shops and factories. There was a beautiful hotel that had cost $150,000 to build. The city owned a steamboat and was planning to build a railroad and a great dam to furnish power for its industries. The gilded spire of a white limestone temple was lifted so high that it could be seen from the Iowa side of the broad Mississippi.

The people who had built Nauvoo called themselves *Latter Day Saints*. Their neighbors called them *Mormons*.

The Mormons loved God, but they had never been able to get along with their neighbors. The frontiersmen who loved the unsettled forests did not like the way hundreds of Mormons came in to the new country, settling in quiet villages and changing the woods and forests into fields and farms. They didn't like the way the Mormons voted together and controlled the elections in any county in which they settled. They thought the Mormons felt that they were better than anybody else because they were "different."

So the Mormons had already had trouble in Ohio and Missouri. And in Illinois a mob had killed Joseph Smith, the first Mormon leader, and his brother, Hyrum.

The leader in 1845 was Brigham Young. He was called *The Lion of the Lord* because of his endless energy and his tawny hair. Frontiersmen in the towns near Nauvoo didn't like the Lion of the Lord any more than they had liked Joseph Smith.

In April Governor Ford of Illinois wrote a letter to Brigham Young. He wrote that he had found the Mormons a peaceful, industrious, law-abiding people. But, he said, he could not promise them protection from their neighbors who might kill them and destroy their property. "If you can get off by yourselves you may enjoy peace; but surrounded by such neighbors, I confess that I do not foresee the time when you will be permitted to enjoy quiet... California now offers a field for the prettiest enterprises that have been undertaken in modern times. It is but sparsely settled... Why would it not be a pretty operation for your people to go out to this vacant country? You would remain there a long time before you would be disturbed by other settlements."

In Quincy, Illinois, there was a noisy mass meeting. The people agreed that they didn't like the Mormons and wanted Brigham Young and his people to leave the state. They sent a committee to meet with the Mormons. The committee told Brigham Young and his counselors that the only thing for them to do was obey the public will and leave Nauvoo as soon as possible. The advice was accompanied by a threat to "use force" if the Mormons didn't leave of their own free will.

Brigham Young listened to the committee. He said, "Since public feeling is aroused against us we will leave as soon as we can sell our property. We will try to sell everything that we hold dear here in Illinois before next spring. Will you help us to get a reasonable price for our factories and shops, our farms, our homes?"

"We will see that no mob harms you," the people of

Quincy promised. "We'll help you to get a reasonable price for your property."

"We must leave our beautiful city," Brigham Young told his people. "We must go west and find a place where we will have no angry neighbors to kill us and destroy our property."

Joseph Smith had dreamed of moving his people across the western plains. He had studied the maps of the great explorers, Lewis and Clark, and the accounts written by fur traders and trappers. He had even selected a group of men to explore and map a Mormon trail.

Now that Brigham Young was the leader he felt that he must make Joseph Smith's dreams come true. Day after day he and his counselor, Heber Kimball, studied maps and searched for a safe route west.

Brigham Young knew that in the great plains there were Indians who had been mistreated by the white men. These Indians were angry and would be dangerous to wagon trains crossing their territory. He knew that the trip across the plains was a long one and that the people and their animals would need food and water. He realized that it would not be easy to cross the Rocky Mountains with the big, awkward wagons and the slow-moving oxen.

Every time he looked out over the beautiful, busy city

of Nauvoo he thought of how the people had worked for eight years to build it; of how they loved their homes, their orchards, their farms.

When he lifted his eyes to the golden spire of the temple they all had worked so hard and sacrificed so much to build, he knew how it would hurt to walk away and leave it.

As he planned the westward migration he remembered that many of the people of Nauvoo were from the mines and the mills of England. Many were quiet farmers and shopkeepers from the sober little towns of New England and upper New York state. How would these people know how to get along on an endless journey west?

In the early days of our country a few men had sometimes joined together to move their families from the seaboard settlements into the Ohio Valley. Later many families made up a wagon train to cross the great plains and the mountains to Oregon. But now Brigham Young had to plan to move not a dozen families, or a hundred, but twenty-five thousand people. And more were arriving every day from New York City, from New England, from Canada, and from England.

Brigham Young was a brave and energetic man. But still the job seemed impossible.

THE GOOD SHIP *BROOKLYN*

Brigham Young was worried about the people in the East who planned to move to Nauvoo. He sent Governor Ford's letter to the Mormons in New York City. He asked Sam Brannon, who published a Mormon newspaper, to print the letter so that everyone could read it. When Sam read the letter he was excited. He loved action and he liked to carry out big, dangerous schemes.

"Crossing the plains to the West is a long, hard journey," he told his counselor, Orson Pratt. "There is a much better way for the Saints from the eastern coast to go to California. Why shouldn't we all go by ship?"

The more Sam thought of taking the Mormons west by ship the better he liked the idea. His black eyes snapped with excitement.

Soon Orson Pratt called all of the people together for a conference. When Sam told the people that he planned to charter a ship to take everyone who wanted to go to California, his words hypnotized his audience. He told the people to use money they had saved to go to Nauvoo for ship's fare to California. He explained that on a ship they could carry heavy machinery, tons of seeds, their chickens and farm stock, even schoolbooks, paper, and the printing press. He asked those who wanted to go to sign their names and put down a deposit.

Many people said that they wanted to go, but they were slow to bring Sam the necessary money.

While the New York Saints sold their property and bought the supplies they would need for the trip West, Sam went up and down the waterfront looking for a ship he could charter. It had to be cheap and it had to be seaworthy. He even went as far as Boston searching for just the right ship. Finally he found a sailing vessel, the Good Ship *Brooklyn*. Captain Richardson said that he would charter the ship for fifteen hundred dollars a month, money in hand before the ship sailed.

Sam Brannon whistled. This was much more than he had planned to pay. Finally he said, "Would you take us for less if I got you a good cargo?"

Captain Richardson said, "If you get me a cargo for the Sandwich Islands (Hawaii), I'll cut the charge to twelve hundred."

Sam was successful in getting the cargo of freight for the Islands. He told Captain Richardson to be ready to sail by the first of February.

Getting ready for this ocean voyage was not an easy task for anyone. The Captain would furnish the food for himself and his crew, but each family must take its own food supplies for the trip. Folks didn't know what to buy for such a voyage. They bought what seemed cheap and likely to keep for several months.

They needed to pack clothing and their own bedding. They had to put their chickens in crates and arrange for the passage of their cows and pigs and horses.

Loading the *Brooklyn* was like Noah loading his ark. Such bellowing and squealing and cackling and mooing had seldom been heard on the docks. Folks stood by to see the plows and harrows, the blacksmith's forge and bellows, the millstones, and the great printing press all swung aboard with a crane and packed away in the hold.

They were surprised to see the boxes of books—179 volumes of Harper's *Family Library* and many schoolbooks besides.

When the ship was all ready to sail Sam heard that the government would try to stop the boat. California was a part of Mexico and Mexico and the United States had a treaty that they would not invade the other's territory.

Sam hoisted a flag which said *Oregon*, and the ship sailed away.

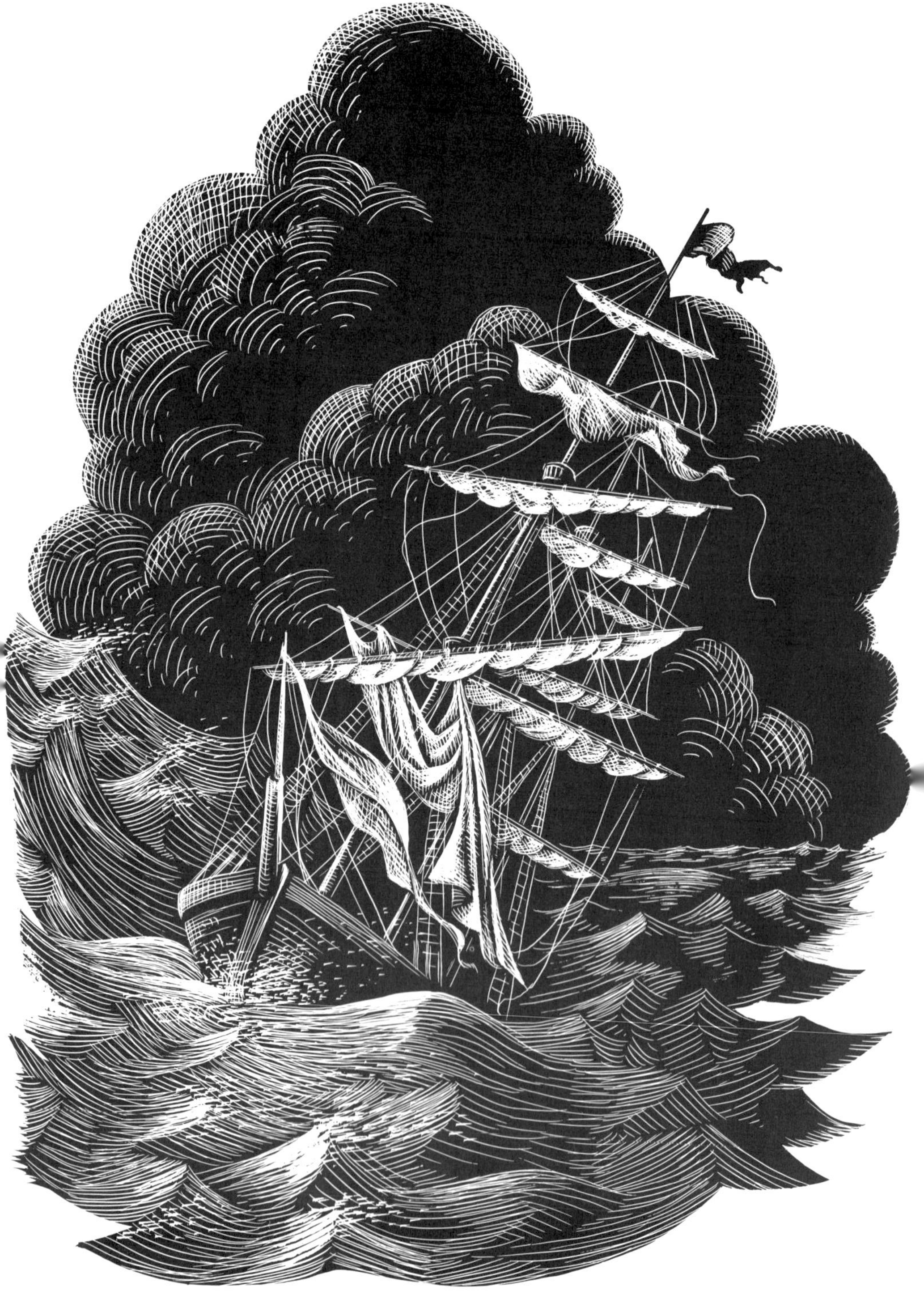

It took some time for the people to get used to the boat. The cabins were very small but there was a large center room where the Saints could hold their meetings in time of storm and where they could eat their meals together. Sam gave each passenger something to do. The crew was hired to operate the ship. The passengers had to keep it clean, help the cook, serve the food, look after the animals.

On Sunday the passengers put on their Sunday clothes and went to a church service held on deck in good weather, in the big room in time of storm.

On the evening of the third day out the wind began to howl. Before night the ship was bucking great waves. Everyone was ordered below and the hatches were battened down. The animals, frightened by the plunging of the ship, began to bellow and squeal and the eerie sound was carried by the gale.

During the night Sam was thrown from his bunk. His wife landed on top of him and his mother-in-law rolled across the floor. Sam tied the women and his little son, Sammy, to their beds.

In the morning when he went to the big room he found only children and young people there waiting for breakfast. Sam sat at the table and prayed. He reminded God that they were in danger and needed His special care. He reminded God that Jesus had said to the waves, "Peace, be still," and the storm had subsided. Finally he said, "Our lives are in Your hands and if it is Thy will that we reach a new Zion, it will be so. Amen."

After the prayer they all joined in singing. Captain Richardson opened the hatch and came down the narrow ladder. He did not speak until the hatch had been closed again because he couldn't have been heard above the snarling of the storm. "We may not outride this storm," he said. "Our ship is taking a fearful beating. It may go down."

The children began to cry.

Sam said, "The Captain is doing his duty in telling us this. What he doesn't know is that we are God's people and God will take care of us." Then he turned to Captain Richardson. "Jesus asked God to still the waters and God did. He'll do the same for us when He is ready."

Captain Richardson didn't say a word. He turned, climbed up the ladder and signaled for the hatch to be opened for him.

For three days the storm lasted, but none of the passengers were really afraid as long as Sam Brannon knew that everything would be all right.

When the storm was over Captain Richardson called

Sam to the ship's bridge. He gave Sam the binoculars. "See that land," Captain Richardson said. "It's the Cape Verde Islands off the coast of Africa."

"What!" Sam exclaimed. "We start for California and end in Africa!"

"We were blown that far from our course," Captain Richardson said.

After the Saints had scrubbed the ship and put everything in order the trip went like a dream. There were meals together prepared by the good cook and his helper, services on Sunday, singing and dancing, to break the monotony, and even the blessing of a baby born on the ship.

In April the Saints began to get sick with scurvy. They hadn't known what supplies to buy and they hadn't brought any fresh fruit or vegetables. The Captain had brought lemons for his crew and Sam ate with the Captain so that they could make plans for the company while they were eating. Sam didn't get sick, but he grieved as one after another of the company got the disease. Six little children died as the ship neared the tip of South America.

Ever since the voyage had begun the Captain and the crew had been worrying about rounding the Horn.

They had worried for nothing. The folks on the deck could see the huge floating islands of ice and feel the chill winds blowing across their faces, but the ship was never in danger. Now the ship was in the Pacific and began its northward voyage.

Captain Richardson promised Sam that the ship would put in at Valparaiso, Chile, for food and water. If Sam could buy fresh fruit and vegetables the Saints who had the scurvy could get better. But as they neared Valparaiso a three-day storm struck the ship. It was carried so far off its course that it was impossible to stop at Valparaiso. Instead the Captain anchored at Robinson Crusoe's Island, an island called Mas-a-tierra.

On this island there were just eight people, four grownups and four children. Once there had been a large colony, but two terrific earthquakes and a raid of Peruvians had killed the people or frightened them away. There were melons and apples and cherries. There were turnips and other vegetables. There were fish of all kinds in the bay and the water was clear and sweet. The crew put 18,000 gallons of water aboard.

The island people were friendly and urged the Saints to take anything they needed during the week they rested there.

After a week the sails took the wind and the ship sailed toward Honolulu. The children studied their lessons on the deck and the grownups did their work or chatted together.

On the 25th of June, 1846, the ship sailed into Honolulu Bay. Here it would stay for a week while the cargo was taken off and new supplies were loaded. Here was a beautiful island, and the Mormons told each other that California could not be more beautiful than this.

The third day in Honolulu the United States frigate, *Congress*, put into the bay. Captain Stockton talked with Sam and told him that the United States and Mexico would soon be at war if war had not already started. He suggested that the *Brooklyn*, whose flag still said *Oregon*, should put in at California. He advised Sam to buy arms in Honolulu so that he could assist in winning California for the United States.

Sam bought muskets for three or four dollars apiece. Soon he had his men drilling under two men who had been in the army. On the Fourth of July, 1846, this ragged little company fired a military salute in honor of the day. Sam planned to reach California before San Francisco Bay had been won by the United States. When the *Brooklyn* sailed into the harbor of San Francisco Bay the stars and stripes were already flying over the tiny, sleepy town.

For five months the Saints had been on the water. Four adults and six children had died. Two babies had been born: a boy named Atlantic and a girl named Pacific. It was August 1, 1846, and the Mormons had arrived at Yerba Buena, the town which would later be called San Francisco.

At first the Saints lived in tents, but very soon they began to build adobe houses similar to those that the Spanish had built all through California. Sam went on an exploring trip up the San Joaquin River and selected a place for a community farm. With money that belonged to the whole group he bought a launch, some oxen, some more seed. Twenty men were sent to the farm to have it in readiness when the Saints under Brigham Young should come on from Nauvoo. The settlement was called *New Hope*.

On January 9th Sam published the first copy of *The California Star*. It was not the first newspaper in the English language published in California. Already there was a small paper called *The Californian* published in Monterey.

At once Sam began to use his paper for the good of the people. The Mormons wanted their children to be in school. Sam pushed the movement to build a school and even printed his offer to give land and fifty dollars toward the project.

In April Sam started his trip across the mountains and deserts to meet Brigham Young and tell him of wonderful California. The first night he and his companions stopped at New Hope. Eighty acres of wheat were already heading out. There would be food for Brigham Young's followers when they arrived in California. There were potatoes, carrots, tomatoes, peas. The men had worked out a system of irrigation to keep the crops growing during the dry summer. For meat they had antelope, deer, bear, geese and ducks.

From there Sam and his companions passed through the mountains, crossed the Oregon Trail at Fort Hall and continued east. Sam's mind was full of beautiful dreams as he hurried to meet Brigham Young. He would tell Brigham Young about the fine bay, about the city that was already alive and growing, about the beautiful farm at New Hope. He would bring all of the Mormon Pioneers to California where they would build a city more beautiful than Nauvoo and where they would soon spread out to occupy the whole of California.

TWENTY THOUSAND PEOPLE MOVE

Brigham Young sat at his desk in Nauvoo. Before him were the maps of the great West. He could hear the hammers ringing as the men built wagon boxes. He could hear the blows of the blacksmith as he made the rims for the wagon wheels. Everyone was feeling restless ever since Governor Ford had advised the Mormons to leave Illinois.

The people in Quincy and the other nearby towns had not kept their promise to help the Saints to sell their property for a reasonable price; still they were threatening to use force if the Mormons didn't leave Nauvoo very soon. Brigham Young had signed an agreement with the citizens' committees of these towns. The Saints would cross the Mississippi in early summer if the mobs would leave them alone while they prepared for the journey west.

"We will divide the Saints into companies of one hundred," Brigham Young told his counselor, Heber Kimball. "We will put a captain over each hundred. These captains can help the members of their companies to outfit their wagons. They can teach them to trade their treasures for sure-footed oxen. The captains can divide the hundreds into companies of ten and put a captain over each ten. In this way every family will be responsible to a captain of ten, a captain of a hundred, and to me."

The people did not want to leave Nauvoo but they did not murmur. By summer they would be ready to begin their journey into nowhere.

But in February, when it was twelve degrees below zero, word came to Nauvoo that Brigham Young was to be arrested and taken away.

All up and down the Mississippi River, in all of the river towns, men who wanted to make money fast had been printing their own money. Some of these counterfeiters had moved into Nauvoo, but Brigham Young had found out about them and had made them leave town. He hated lawlessness and dishonesty. But now he was accused of being a counterfeiter, himself. He knew that he was innocent but he didn't want to be tried for any crime by people who hated him and were eager to hurt him and his people.

"We cannot wait until summer," Brigham Young told his followers. "We must move now."

Before he left, Brigham Young and the leading men in Nauvoo held a meeting in the temple. They signed the Nauvoo Covenant. "We covenant this day that we (will) take all our Saints with us, to the extent of our ability, that is our influence and property." This meant that all of the people of Nauvoo placed their money, their wagons, everything that they possessed at the disposal of a committee of the "Camp of Israel." Brigham Young was chairman of the committee. Later he was to take wagons from those who had two so that the poor could join the exodus. He was to use the money of those who were well off to help those who were poor.

The Mississippi River was covered with ice. Two thousand Mormons used the ice as a bridge to cross from Illinois into Iowa.

"Our enemies will be satisfied now that we have started to leave Nauvoo," Brigham Young told his followers.

But he had not guessed right. Twenty-three thousand Saints still lived in the city. "We've got the Mormons on the run," the neighbors said, feeling stronger and braver. "Let's help them to hurry!"

So when the Saints went out of the city to work on their farms their neighbors shot at them. Some men were kidnapped and whipped. One man was hanged and left until he nearly strangled, then he was cut down. Very few men would buy the houses and farms and factories in

Nauvoo. "We can have these things for nothing when the Mormons are driven out," the neighbors said.

Even though the weather was still freezing cold and the people were not ready to make the long journey, the wagons began moving westward in companies of one hundred.

Brigham Young had established a camp on Sugar Creek in Iowa. It was called "The Camp of Israel." Here every wagon was stopped and inspected. Every family had to take seed grain and farm implements. Every wagon and team had to be sound. Not one could start across the plains until the committee saw that he was properly outfitted. Pigs and poultry had to be in pens fastened to the wagons. Sheep, cattle, cows, mules and horses could be driven with the company herd.

By May there were wagons scattered all along the western trail from the shores of the Mississippi River to the banks of the Missouri. Twenty thousand people were on the march.

Things got harder and harder for the last Saints to leave Nauvoo. This little remnant was made up of the old, the sick, the very poor who had not been able to get an outfit together. The mobs made life unbearable for them. When Brigham Young heard of their plight he sent wagons

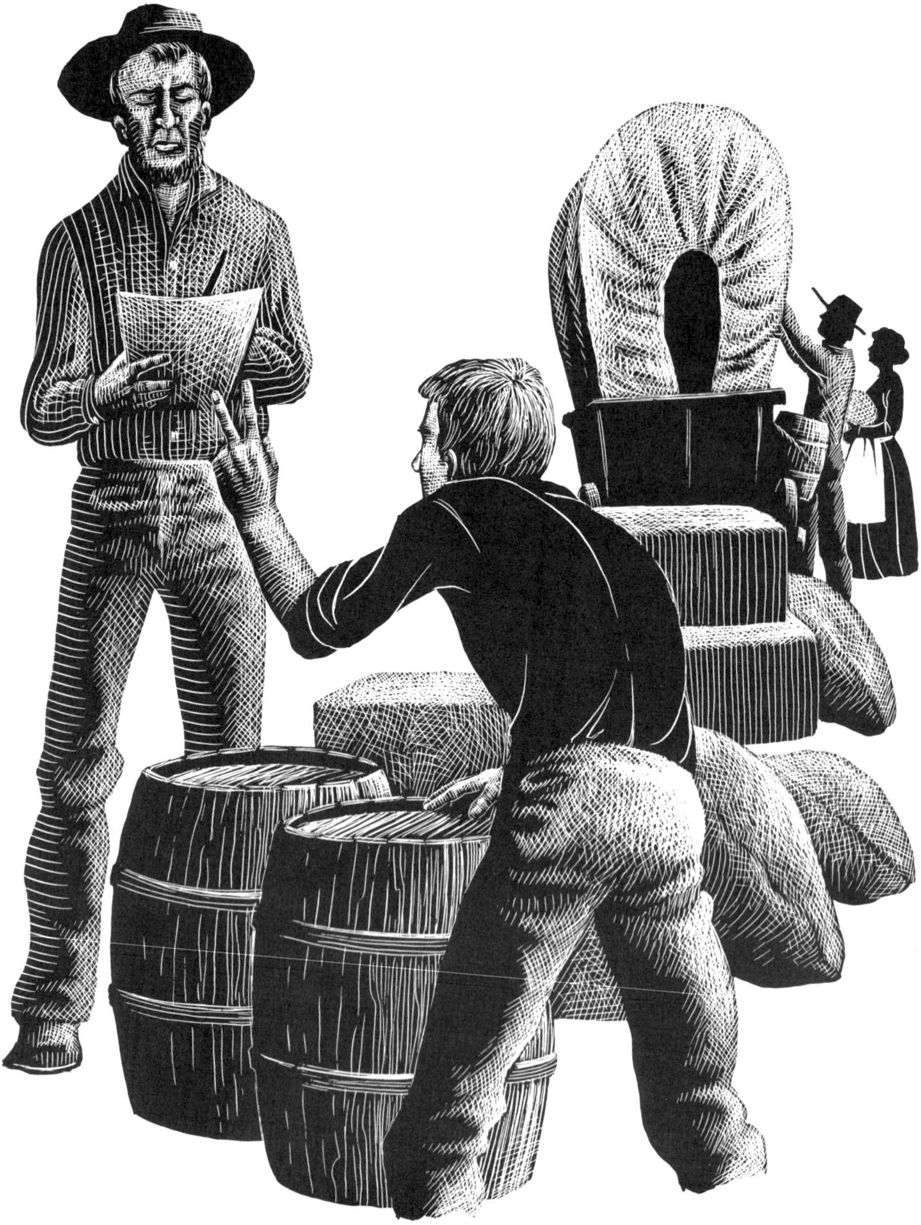

back for them. It was late summer when this last pitiful company looked across the river to their beautiful city. Someone had set fire to barns, and it looked as if the whole city were in flames. Even the temple had been fired by a man who had climbed up into the spire.

"We can never return to our homes," the Mormons said. "We must follow Brigham Young to the west."

"How will all of these people live?" Heber Kimball asked Brigham Young. "We do not have just this twenty thousand to worry about. Others are coming from the East and from faraway England. They will plan to get supplies in Nauvoo. They will not know that Nauvoo is in the hands of our enemies."

"I have a plan," Brigham Young said. "Our people are fine farmers. We will send twenty-five men, called *pioneers*, ahead of the company to plant patches of grain that later travelers can harvest. When it is time to prepare the soil for crops, a company of one hundred can stop and plow; then it can move on. When it is time to plant the seed, another company of a hundred can put in the seed. God will send the rain to bring our crops to maturity. Then another company can harvest the crop. We will make some permanent camps so that all the Saints may be supplied as they cross Iowa. We will leave blacksmiths and carpenters in these camps to mend the wagons that fall to pieces on the march."

These were excellent plans but they did not help the Saints in the first companies. "We are cold. We are hungry. Our babies are being born in our wagons, on the ground under the wagons, in shelters made by throwing a blanket over posts driven into the ground. What shall we do?" the people asked.

"Be of good cheer," Brigham Young said. "We will sing. Singing will lift our hearts and make all things possible to us."

William Clayton, who had come from England, wrote the marching song:

> *Come, come, ye Saints,*
> *No toil nor labor fear,*
> *But with joy wend your way;*
> *Though hard to you*
> *The journey may appear*
> *Grace shall be, as your day.*
> *'Tis better far for us to strive*
> *Our useless cares from us to drive;*
> *Do this, and joy your hearts will swell.*
> *All is well! All is well!*

When the Mormons made camp at night the men set up the tents and started fires burning while the women

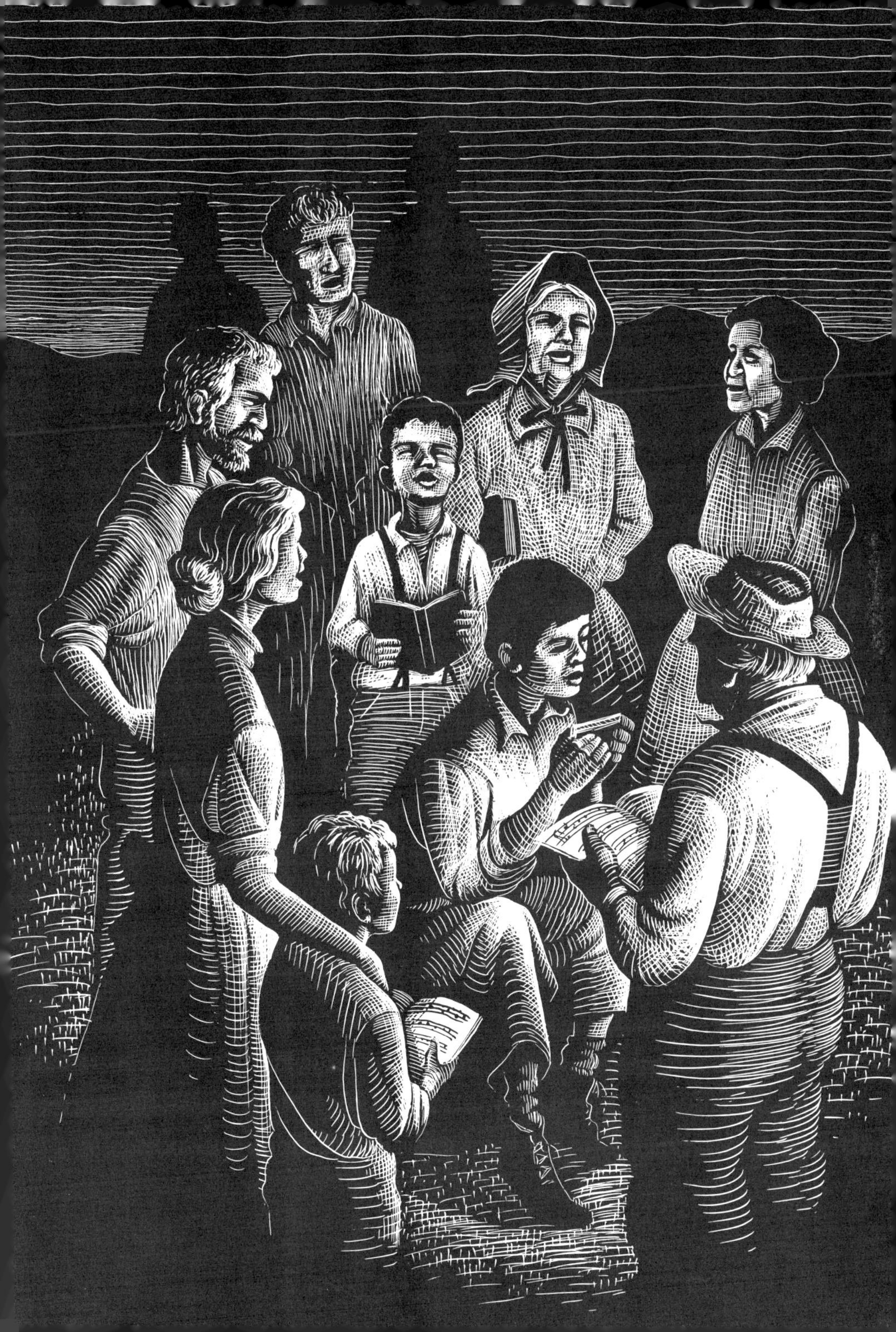

prepared the evening meal. Always there was singing after supper. Often there was dancing.

"If we do not keep our spirits up we will die," they said. So they danced on tired feet and sang with tired voices, "Come, Come, ye Saints."

In June Brigham Young crossed the Missouri River. He had traveled three and a half months and covered about one hundred miles each month.

"We cannot go further," Brigham Young told Heber Kimball. "Many miles are before us and winter would overtake us before we crossed the Rocky Mountains. Besides we must wait here for those who are still near the Mississippi."

"We are on the border of Indian territories," Brother Kimball said. "What shall we do now? Must we fight Indians?"

"The Indians know what it means to be treated as we have been treated by our neighbors. Their chief is Big Elk. I will speak with him."

Big Elk was surprised when Brigham Young came to his camp to speak with him. The Indians had not met this kind of white man before.

Brigham Young stood before the tall dark Indian as calm as if he were talking to Brother Kimball in his own tent. "We are on a journey to California," he told the chief. "With your permission we would like to winter here. We can do you good. We will repair your guns and make a farm for you. We will aid you in any other way that we can. We should like to have some of your honorable young men watch our cattle. Will your young men keep our cattle safe? Have you any objection to our getting timber, building houses, and staying here until spring or longer?"

Big Elk was silent.

Brigham Young went on, "The government is willing if you are. Will you be our friends? Are you willing that we should sow wheat here this year and plant corn next spring? I will be glad to have you say what is in your heart."

Big Elk replied, "My son, thou hast spoken well. I have all that thou hast said in my heart. I have much I want to say. We are poor. When we go to hunt game in one place our enemies kill us. We do not kill them. I hope we will be friends. You may stay on these lands two years or more. Our young men may watch your cattle. We would be glad to trade with you. We will warn you of danger from other Indians."

After Brigham Young went back to his camp he heard someone grumbling, "We are already hungry. How can we help these Indians?"

Brigham Young said, "It is better to feed the Indians than to fight them."

HUNGRY, FOOTSORE BATTALION

The Mormons made their winter quarters at Council Bluffs. One day an army officer rode into camp.

"The United States is at war," the army officer told Brigham Young. "We are fighting Mexico. Our government wants you to supply a Mormon battalion of five hundred young men to march into Mexican territory."

Brigham Young was silent. Five hundred young men! If five hundred young men left, who would serve as scouts? Who would be teamsters? Who would build the roads and bridges? Who would take care of the wives and children of these men?

"The government will pay part of the salary of these men before they leave. The government will give them food and clothing for their journey west. The men will be discharged near the new settlement you plan to make in the West."

"We will furnish five hundred men," Brigham Young said. "If we do not have enough young men we will send old men. If we do not have enough men we will send the women."

There were not five hundred young men in Winter Quarters. Taking two friends with him, Brigham Young started back along the trail. Whenever he met with the Saints pushing westward, he stopped and talked with them. "This is a good prospect for our deliverance," he said. "If we do not take it we are doomed."

Very soon the five hundred young men were ready to march away. Before the Mormon Battalion left Council Bluffs, Brigham Young talked to the officers.

"Officers, be as fathers to the privates. Remember your prayers; see that the name of Deity is revered; that virtue and cleanliness are strictly observed. Treat all men with kindness. Never take that which does not belong to you even from your worst enemies, not even in time of war. In case you come in contact with your enemies and defeat them, treat the prisoners with kindness and never take life when it can be avoided."

Then Brigham Young stopped talking and looked far out over the heads of the officers to where the men were gathering. "If you will go forth and be true to your country and to God I promise you that you shall not be required to shed blood and there will not be a bullet fired at you."

All of the Saints at Council Bluffs waved good-by to

the Battalion as it started south along the banks of the Missouri River.

This was a strange army. Some of the soldiers marched as they sang *The Girl I Left Behind Me*. Some rode on their own mules. Some even rode in their own wagons with their wives and children.

It did not take long for some of the marchers to grow tired. In five days they traveled thirty-eight miles in the heat and dust. They had been promised that the government would give them good food, but already the flour had been used and the first real stop, Fort Leavenworth, was still more than a hundred and fifty miles away.

But every man did his best and Colonel Allen said, "You are good soldiers. I have never had to give an order twice."

At Fort Leavenworth it was 101° in the shade and 135° in the sun. The men were in the sun! They pitched new tents and felt, for the first time, like a real army.

When the men were mustered in, every man could sign his own name on the roll. The officers at Fort Leavenworth were surprised. Of the recruits who had been mustered in the day before, only one out of three had been able to write his name.

Colonel Allen looked at the Mormon Battalion. "This

is not an army," he said. "We are going to march two thousand miles. Already some of you are tired and sick. The sick men must not try to make the march with us. They must go to a fort called Pueblo on the Arkansas River. The women and children must go to Pueblo, too. This will be too hard a journey for women and children."

The sick men, the children, and most of the women started for Pueblo. The men who had ridden in their own wagons now marched with the others. Colonel Allen was sick. He stayed at Fort Leavenworth while the Battalion began the long, long journey.

Very soon the men were glad that their families had not started on the march. Word came to them that Colonel Allen had died. A cross officer, Lieutenant Smith, took his place.

Everybody was thirsty and there was no water. Finally they came to a lake. Everybody was happy until a herd of buffalo was seen bathing in the lake. The Battalion drank the water anyway. They had marched twenty-five miles without a drink.

The bad water made some of the men sick, but they did not report that they were sick because they were afraid of Dr. Sanderson. He was a gruff man with a great big, rusty iron spoon. The sick men lined up and he gave each

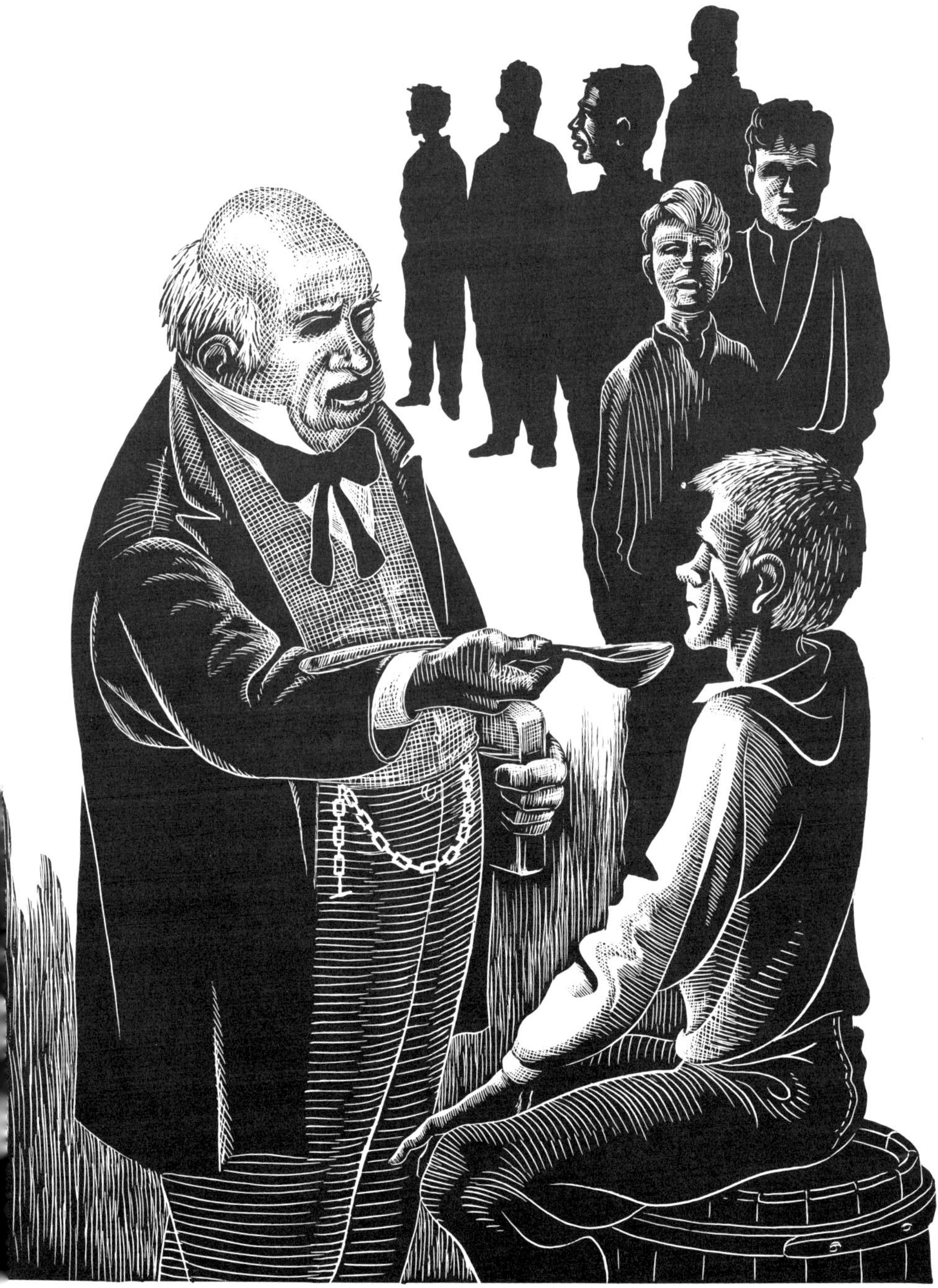

of them a spoonful of calomel and arsenic. He didn't bother to find out what sickness they had.

There was not enough food and men were living on two-thirds rations. The Battalion moved more and more slowly.

One day word came to the camp that the Mexicans had given up Santa Fe. The strongest men in the Battalion were to hurry on to Santa Fe while the sick ones were to come along as fast as they could. Dr. Sanderson went with the well soldiers and left the sick soldiers to take care of themselves.

As the Battalion came closer to Santa Fe both the food and water got better. But still some were too tired and sick to travel. From Santa Fe Captain Brown took all of the women but five, and all of the sick men back to Pueblo.

Colonel Cooke took command of the Battalion. The men were happy to get away from the cross Lieutenant Smith.

After the Battalion left Santa Fe the route got harder. The men carried blankets, knapsacks, cartridge boxes containing thirty-six rounds of ammunition, and their muskets. They were weak from being poorly fed.

Colonel Cooke said, "These mules and oxen are hungry and thirsty. See how thin and tired they are. They cannot pull the supply wagons. You must help them."

The men pulled on long ropes to help the mules and oxen pull the supply wagons through the quicksand. Sometimes the men leaned against the wheels of the wagons to help the wagons move forward. They were tired, but they could sing.

> *Put your shoulder to the wheel, push along,*
> *Do your duty with a heart full of song.*
> *We all have work; let no one shirk;*
> *Put your shoulder to the wheel.*

Sometimes they sang a sad song:

> *Our hardships reach their rough extremes*
> *When valiant men are roped with teams*
> *Hour after hour and day by day*
> *To wear our strength and lives away.*
>
> *We, some twenty men or more*
> *With empty stomachs and footsore*
> *Bound to one wagon, plodding on*
> *Through sand beneath the burning sun.*
>
> *How hard to starve and wear us out*
> *Upon this sandy desert route.*

Finally the Battalion reached the place where General Kearney, the top general in California, had left his wagons and pushed on with pack animals. He had left orders for the Mormon Battalion to open a wagon road from Santa Fe to the Pacific Ocean.

It was no surprise to anybody that General Kearney had left his wagons. The Battalion took six days to travel forty miles over the rough, broken country. More of the men gave out. Fifty-five were sent back to Pueblo to join the sick.

"We have very little food left," Colonel Cooke said. "We have five days' rations to feed us while we travel three hundred miles. We must travel lighter. We will leave our cooking utensils, our tent poles, some of our tents and two of our wagons."

"How can we put up our tents at night?" the soldiers asked.

"You will use your muskets for tent poles. You must not throw away your muskets."

From this time on not even the guides knew the way. The men tramped in double file in front of the wagons, just far enough apart to make trails for the wheels. The men took turns at this hard work.

Still everybody was thirsty and water was scarce. Once, after the men had been forty-eight hours without water, the advance guide came to a little spring. The officers decided that the animals needed a drink more than the men did and allowed the animals to drink first.

The soldiers were glad to begin climbing the Rocky Mountains because although there was less food for the animals, there were more springs of fresh water.

Going down the west side of the mountains was harder than climbing the east side. The wagons had to be lowered over the cliffs with ropes. The animals were packed and led down one at a time. But there were beautiful sights to look at and sparkling rivers flowing westward.

In Tucson there were two hundred Mexican soldiers. The Mormon Battalion was too tired to fight even two hundred mice! Word reached Tucson that the Mormon Battalion was the advance guard of a great army. The Mexican soldiers and most of the people ran away.

The Mormon Battalion remembered Brigham Young's words. They did not take any of the food and clothing that belonged to the people. They took 2,000 pounds of wheat that belonged to the Mexican Government.

After the Battalion left Tucson the men were again without water for days at a time. One afternoon they came to a spring so small that the officers wouldn't let the men dip for a drink. They could lie on their stomachs and drink from the pools and puddles or not drink at all.

At last the Battalion, now with 360 members, reached the Gila (Heela) River. Here the Indians were honest and kind. The soldiers cut the buttons from their clothing and traded the buttons for food.

But after the army started along the Gila River the Colonel ordered the men to carry the food they had got from the Indians or else leave it on the ground. Starving men, too weak to carry heavier loads, left their food on the ground.

Now the army pushed on over the hardest part of the trail. When the animals gave out they were killed and eaten. The meat was always boiled and the men used the two spoonfuls of flour they received each day, to thicken the gravy. Those who were lucky enough to get the insides of the animals broiled them on a stick over the fire. Even the hides, after the hair had been burned off, was cut into pieces and boiled until it was tender enough to chew.

"There are not enough animals left to pull the wagons," Captain Cooke said. "We will fasten two wagons together to make a barge and float our supplies down the river."

"Do not do that," the men begged. "The river is wider and shallower here. There will be sand bars. Everything will be lost."

The officers did not listen to the men. They made

two wagons into a barge. Often the barge was stuck on sand bars. Each time more provisions had to be left. Rations were now reduced to one ounce of flour each day.

After the Battalion had left the river the men were again without water for two days. The advance guard found an old well that had dried up. They dug it two feet deeper. Water appeared and they all shouted and even cried with happiness. But the water was soon covered with quicksand.

"Bring a washtub," someone cried. "We will fix this well!"

One of the women had a washtub. "You cannot have my washtub," she told the men. "I have carried this tub all the way from Nauvoo."

But later, when she saw men sucking water through a quill, she brought the washtub.

The men made holes in the washtub and put it in the bottom of the well. The water did not come up through the holes. Next they knocked the bottom out of the tub and made it into a wall for the well. This worked for a moment and the men cheered. Then the water disappeared. Now even the strong men had tears in their eyes. They dug the well two feet deeper and water appeared again. This time there was enough to fill the camp kettles.

Now the Battalion moved from one well to the next

one. Sometimes the wells were two days' travel apart. Once there were five days without water. The road was through heavy sands and under a blazing sun. Twenty well-armed men could have defeated the whole Battalion.

Men staggered as they marched. Some wore worn-out shoes; some had old rags wrapped around their feet; some had slipped their feet into a section of ox hide cut from the back leg of the animal. Cut in one piece, the bend of the leg made a natural heel for the strange moccasin.

The last flour rations were eaten. There had been no sugar, coffee, corn or other rations for weeks. A few sheep had been driven along with the Battalion, but they were so thin and hungry and thirsty that they had no meat on their bones when they were slaughtered. All but five of the government wagons had been left behind somewhere along the trail.

Suddenly the Battalion faced a rock ridge two hundred feet high. The men surmounted it. With hand axes they hewed out enough stone to make the passage as wide as the wagons. Even the Commander helped.

Now they dropped down into a beautiful country. There were fat beef cattle here that could be bought for a cent a pound. The men were given four pounds of beef a day, but no other ration, not even salt. Soon the men learned to pick mustard greens in the meadows and buy corn cakes from the Indians.

Six months and nine days from the morning the Bat-

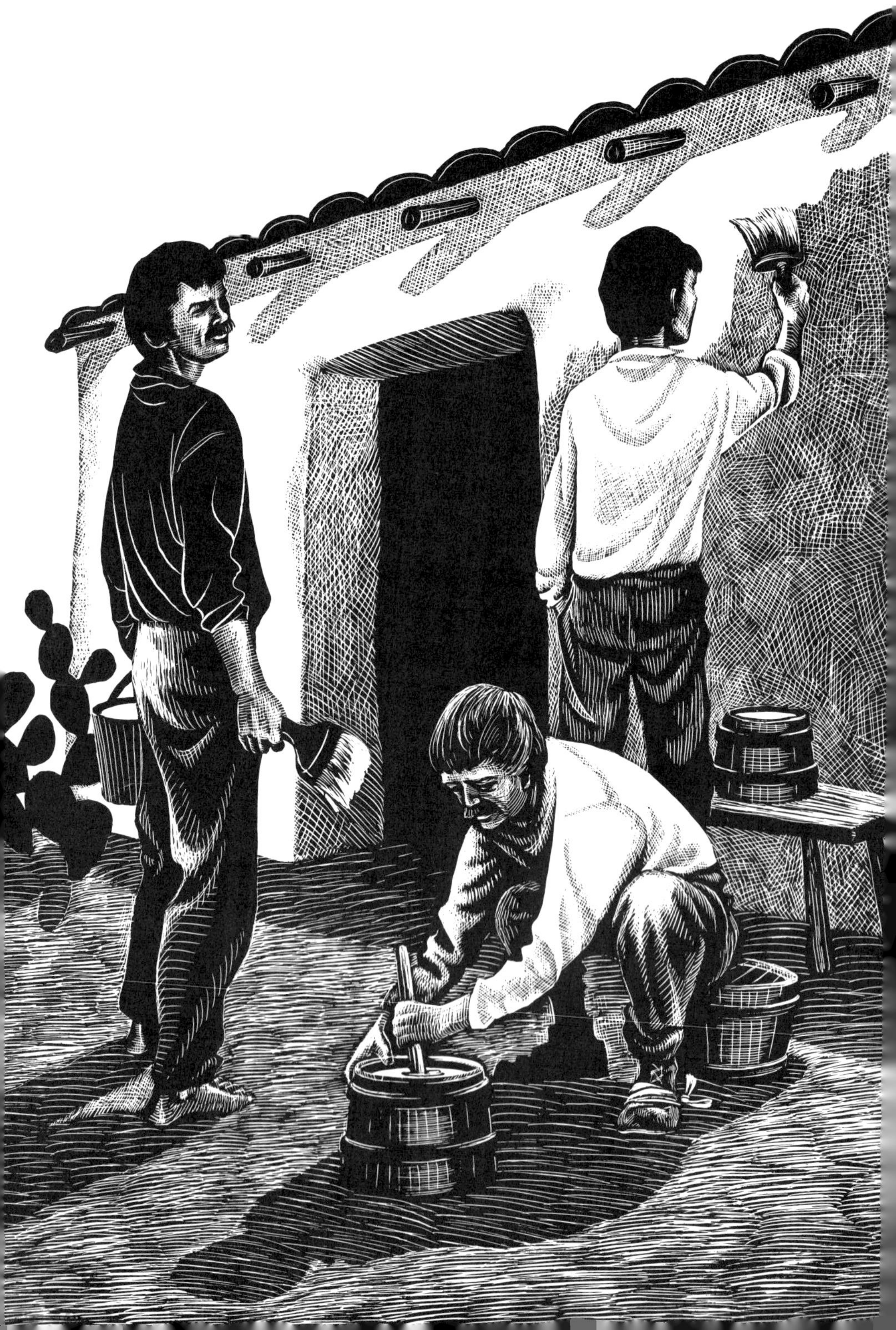

talion had left Council Bluffs, what was left of it arrived in San Diego.

Colonel Cooke said: "History may be searched in vain for an equal march of infantry. Half of it has been through a wilderness where nothing but savages and wild beasts are found, or deserts where, for want of water, there is no living creature. There with almost hopeless labor we have dug wells, which the future traveler will enjoy . . . With crowbar and pickax in hand we have moved over mountains . . . and hewed a chasm of living rock more narrow than our wagons. Thus marching half-naked, half-fed, and living upon wild animals, we have discovered and made a road of great value to our country."

One company of the Mormon Battalion stayed in San Diego to dig wells, make bricks, and to help the people in every way. The rest of the Battalion went to Los Angeles. In Los Angeles they whitewashed buildings, helped turn a sleepy Mexican village into a shining, clean American village and built Forte Moore.

Some of the Mormon Battalion re-enlisted, some went North to join the Mormon colony in San Francisco, some went back to the Salt Lake Valley as soon as possible, and some helped to find gold in Sutter's Creek near Sacramento, California.

VALLEY OF THE GREAT SALT LAKE

After the Mormon Battalion had marched away from Council Bluffs Brigham Young said, "We must cross the Missouri River into Nebraska. The people of Iowa are not our friends. We have asked the government to let us stay on Indian lands. Already the Indians have said that they would be our brothers."

So the Mormons crossed the Missouri River. In Nebraska they built a new town called *Winter Quarters*. The Mormons were good workers. They built sturdy homes, a blacksmith shop, a flour mill, a meeting house, and a school. Around the town they built a stockade to keep the Indians out. They planted gardens and fields of grain.

Although they worked hard from sunup to sunset all the rest of the summer, winter came before they were prepared for it. The weather was cold; there was hunger and sickness. When the people no longer had fresh vegetables from their gardens they got scurvy. Those who had the disease called it "black leg." The legs swelled twice their size and turned black. Many old people who had dragged themselves across Iowa in hopes of reaching "the promised land" gave up and died. Most of the babies died. Every day there was a funeral at some grave side.

But still the people sang:

> *Why should we mourn or think our lot is hard?*
> *'Tis not so; all is right.*
> *Why should we think to earn a great reward*
> *If we now shun the fight?*
>
> *Gird up your loins, fresh courage take.*
> *Our God will never us forsake;*
> *And soon we'll have this tale to tell—*
> *All is well! All is well!*

Brigham Young got thinner and thinner. Much of the time he was sick, but he never stopped working.

There was a cure for "black leg." If there were potatoes to eat the "black leg" went away. Brigham Young sent men all the way back across Iowa to Missouri to bring potatoes for the people in Winter Quarters.

One day a woman found some horseradish growing in an old broken-down fort. She brought the horseradish home. The Mormons found that horseradish was as good as potatoes to cure the "black leg."

In spite of the sickness and death the people sang at their work. They sang and danced in the evenings. They did not complain about the hard life.

As soon as spring came Brigham Young sold his flour

mill. He told the Saints how to take care of their houses, plant their crops, and get along with the Indians. Then he selected some of the Saints to be the first pioneer company. He chose 143 men and boys, three women and two children.

Each man had a rifle and the company took along a small cannon.

"We will not hurt the Indians," Brigham Young said. "If they bother us we will frighten them with the noise from this cannon." In seventy wagons the Mormons packed plows, seed-grain, and provisions to last one year.

One morning the pioneers rode out toward the west. First were the scouts, then the hunters, then Brigham Young. Behind him was the wagon train.

"We will soon follow you," the people called as they waved good-by to the first pioneer company.

Each morning the bugle sounded at five. The men had two hours to prepare their breakfast, eat it, say their morning prayers, and get their animals hooked to their wagons. At seven the wagon train was supposed to be ready to move. Sometimes when someone had been careless the whole train had to wait for one man to find his animals that had been allowed to stray during the night.

During the day the wagons kept close together because

the wagon train might meet unfriendly Indians. Usually the wagons moved single file, but once in Indian country they moved five abreast. The men walked beside their oxen and the sun flashed from their rifle barrels.

At night the wagons were gathered in a close circle. The animals were allowed to graze inside the circle of wagons. Fifty men were guards. Each half-night twelve men watched for dangers.

Fifteen days after they had left Winter Quarters the pioneers saw their first buffalo. Hunters rode after the animals and brought back eleven. The men made Indian jerky by cutting the meat into strips and drying it in the sun.

Four days later the pioneers came upon a band of about four hundred Indians. The pioneers were frightened but they kept their wagons moving toward the west. The Indians followed the wagon train. Brigham Young said, "I do not like these Indians following us. I cannot tell what they will do next. We will fire our cannon. That will frighten them."

The men fired the cannon and the Indians rode away. The Indians were not hurt but they were angry. They set fire to the grass in front of the wagon train. The pioneers had to wait for the wind to carry the flames away from them before they could go on with the journey.

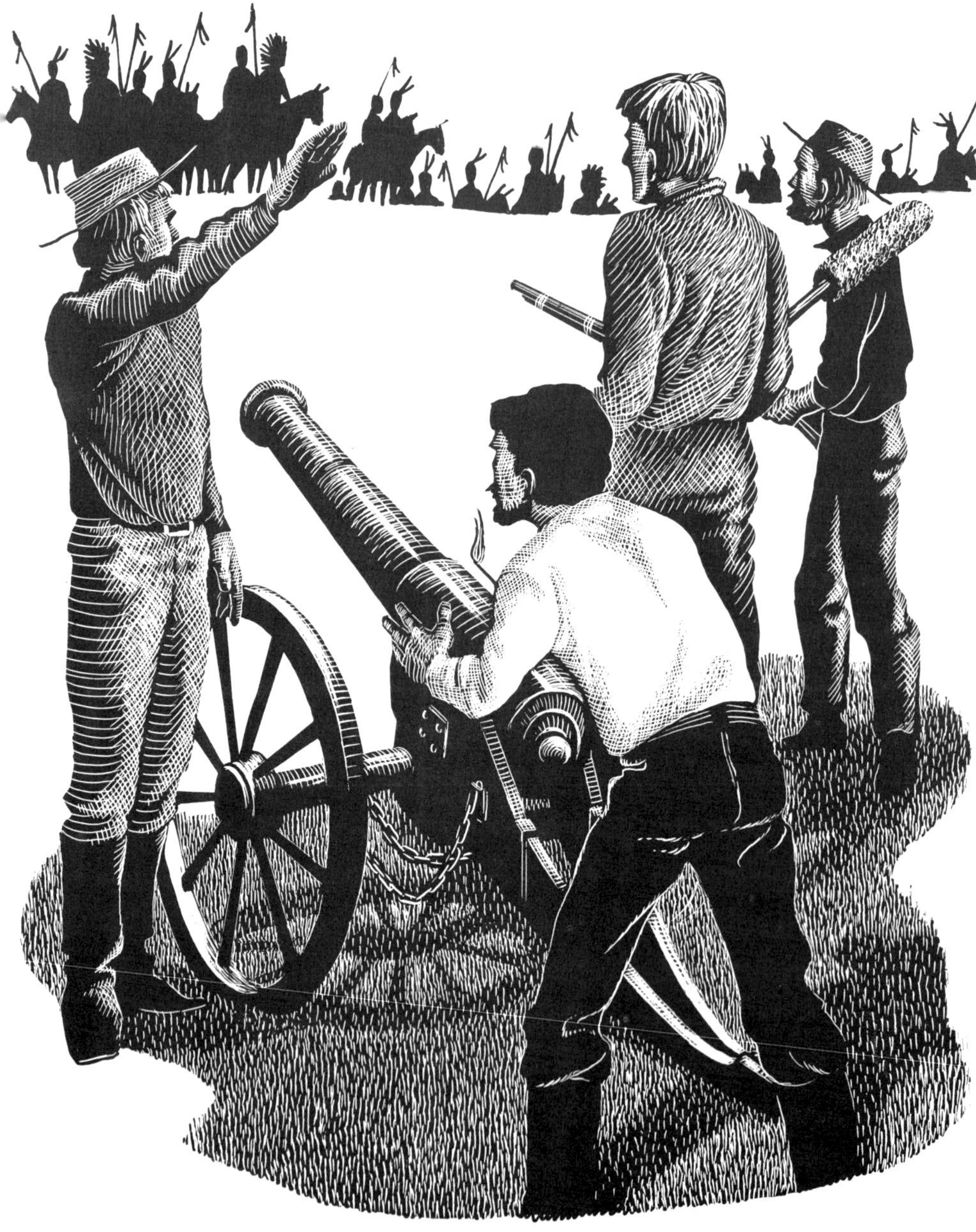

As the wagon train moved slowly along the Platte River it had to stop several times for great herds of buffalo to pass. The young men thought it great fun to hunt the buffalo. They rode their horses around the buffalo herd whooping and hollering and waving their hats. But Brigham Young said, "You must not kill more animals than are needed for meat. God does not want you to waste his blessings."

The Mormon pioneers had been traveling along the road that the Oregon pioneers traveled. Now the Oregon Trail crossed to the south bank of the Platte. The Mormon pioneers kept on the north bank of the river.

"What will those who come after us do? How will they know that we have left the Oregon Trail?" the scouts asked Brigham Young.

"We will write letters and tell those who are following us where we are going," Brigham Young said.

The men wrote long letters. Sometimes they drew maps on the letters. They put the letters in a notch cut in a board; then they nailed the board to a fifteen-foot pole. Sometimes they wrote very short letters. "All is well. June 1," on the bleached skull of a buffalo and left it by the side of the trail.

One day a scout rode into the camp. When the men

saw that the scout was a Mormon who had left with the Mormon Battalion, they gathered around him. "How is my son, Arza?" one asked. Another said, "How is my brother, Rufus?"

The scout said, "The march was too hard for most of the women. It was even too hard for many of the men. All those who could not keep up with the Battalion have spent the winter in Pueblo."

"We know all of that," Brigham Young said impatiently. "Where are the Pueblo Saints now? What are their plans?"

"They have been eager to join you. When you reach Laramie you will find them there ahead of you."

But when Brigham Young and his company reached Fort Laramie the company had not come. Brigham Young waited four days, mending wagons and resting the animals. "Already the green of the grassy plains has changed to the purple of the desert. We must not wait another day. Ahead of us are the Rocky Mountains. See, you can see the snow-capped peaks from here. We must find our way through these mountains. I would like to wait for the Pueblo Saints but instead I will write a letter to tell them to follow us."

The company from Pueblo arrived at Fort Laramie

less than a week later. They read Brigham Young's letter. This company with many women and children could not travel so fast as the first pioneer company; they trailed Brigham Young by a week or more all the rest of the journey.

When the pioneers had gone a hundred miles past Fort Laramie they had to cross to the south side of the Platte River. The Saints had expected to wade through the stream but now they found it flooded with spring rains. They had to find another way to get across. Brigham Young had the men make a boat of buffalo and ox hides stretched over a wood frame. On this leather boat they took their goods across the river.

Some men on the way to Oregon saw the leather boat. "May we use your boat?" they asked Brigham Young. "We will pay you well."

"We will float your supplies across the river for you," Brigham Young said.

"We do not have money. We will pay you with flour," the Oregon travelers said. The Mormons were glad to get the flour!

"We will need a ferry at this point," Brigham Young said. "All of our companies will need help in getting their outfits across the Platte. The Oregon pioneers will need the ferry, too."

The men who operated the boat could see Brigham Young's questioning eyes upon them. They were eager to travel on and be the first men to reach the new land of promise, but they said, "We will stay here and operate this ferry until the river shrinks in the summer heat."

The men with the leather boat watched the pioneer wagon train out of sight.

On the thirtieth day of June, 1847, Sam Brannon rode into Brigham Young's camp on the shore of the Green River near the mouth of the Little Sandy.

Brigham Young was glad to see him. He asked about the Mormon pioneers who had traveled by water on the *Brooklyn*. He asked about what these settlers had done since they landed on San Francisco Bay. Sam's black eyes flashed with eagerness. All the long trip toward the east he had been planning what he would say to Brigham Young.

"San Francisco is a fine town. We have built fifty new homes there. Some are of lumber but some are made of sun-dried brick. You can build a sun-dried brick house in two weeks. We have a beautiful eighty acres in wheat and garden stuff on a navigable river a day's journey from

San Francisco Bay. When I stopped there the grain was already heading out. We will have food for all of you when you arrive."

"We are not going to California," Brigham Young said. "We are going to build our homes in the Valley of the Great Salt Lake."

"But—" began Sam Brannon.

"You may talk and I will listen," Brigham Young said, "but I will not change my mind. The Saints are going to settle where no one else will want to settle. We must be far away from neighbors who will injure us and destroy our property. If we have ten years by ourselves we can become strong enough so that no one can destroy us."

Sam thought of all the work he had done in Yerba Buena and at New Hope. He thought of the beautiful bay and the wide rivers that flowed into it. "California—" he began, but he could see by the closed look on Brigham Young's face that nothing would change his mind. When the company moved on the next day Sam Brannon rode beside Orson Pratt, his friend from the old days in New York City.

Disappointed and angry that a decision should have been made before Brigham Young had even seen what the Saints had accomplished in California, Sam was glad to be assigned to go back over the trail to meet the folks coming from Pueblo and lead them to the Great Salt Lake Valley.

Brigham Young and his company trudged on toward the western mountains. It had been a month and a half since they left the body of the Saints before they reached Fort Bridger. Jim Bridger kept the trading post. "Where are you folks going?" he asked Brigham Young.

"We are going to the Valley of the Great Salt Lake," Brigham Young said.

"Why do you want to take so many people to settle there?" Jim Bridger asked. "It is a barren country. I will give you one thousand dollars for the first bushel of grain that you grow there."

But Brigham Young was not discouraged. He was looking for a place where no other settlers would want to make their homes. He had had enough of angry neighbors.

Soon the Oregon Trail turned off toward the north. Brigham Young and his company of pioneers entered the mountains where no wagon train had ever traveled.

None of the Saints had seen mountains like these before. The peaks were so high that they were still crowned with snow. The trail moved dangerously along the edge of rushing streams. There were rocks underfoot and crags lifted like stone walls hundreds of feet above the heads of the pioneers. Men who had been singing and whistling now were silent. Somehow they felt very much alone, yet God seemed very near.

Brigham Young sent messengers back to tell those who followed which way to go. He sent scouts ahead to find passes through the mountains.

Slowly the pioneer wagon train wound its way through the dangerous mountain passes. "We should soon be through these mountains," Brigham Young said. "I will send scouts ahead to see what the Valley of the Great Salt Lake is like."

On the twenty-fourth of July Brigham Young was sick. Instead of riding at the head of the wagon train he had to rest in Heber Kimball's wagon. When the wagon moved out of a deep canyon he raised himself on his elbow and looked out.

A wide green valley, patched with summer yellow, stretched away to the west. Beyond it was the glistening blue of the Great Salt Lake. And beyond that, hidden by the soft summer haze, other mountains lifted their heads. There was scarcely a tree to be seen, but willows and brush grew along the edges of the streams that crossed the valley from the mouths of the canyons and emptied into the Great Salt Lake.

The scouts had arrived two days before. They had begun to plow the land and had turned the water of the mountain streams out over the thirsty earth. The damp, plow-turned soil made a patch of rich brown on the green-yellow of the valley.

Brigham Young said:

"This is the place! Drive on."

The first pioneer company did not take time to rest after the long journey.

"We must have a place to meet together and praise the Lord," Brigham Young said. "We will build a bowery."

He showed the men who were not busy with plowing the land and planting the seed how to make a roof of fresh-cut willows and boughs from the cottonwood that grew along the banks of the streams. This leafy roof was forty feet long and twenty-eight feet wide. The people sat in its shade on rough-hewn logs for benches.

Five days after Brigham Young had said, "This is the place!" the first company of pioneers went to the mouth of Emigration Canyon to greet the folks from Pueblo whom they had missed at Fort Laramie. The band played

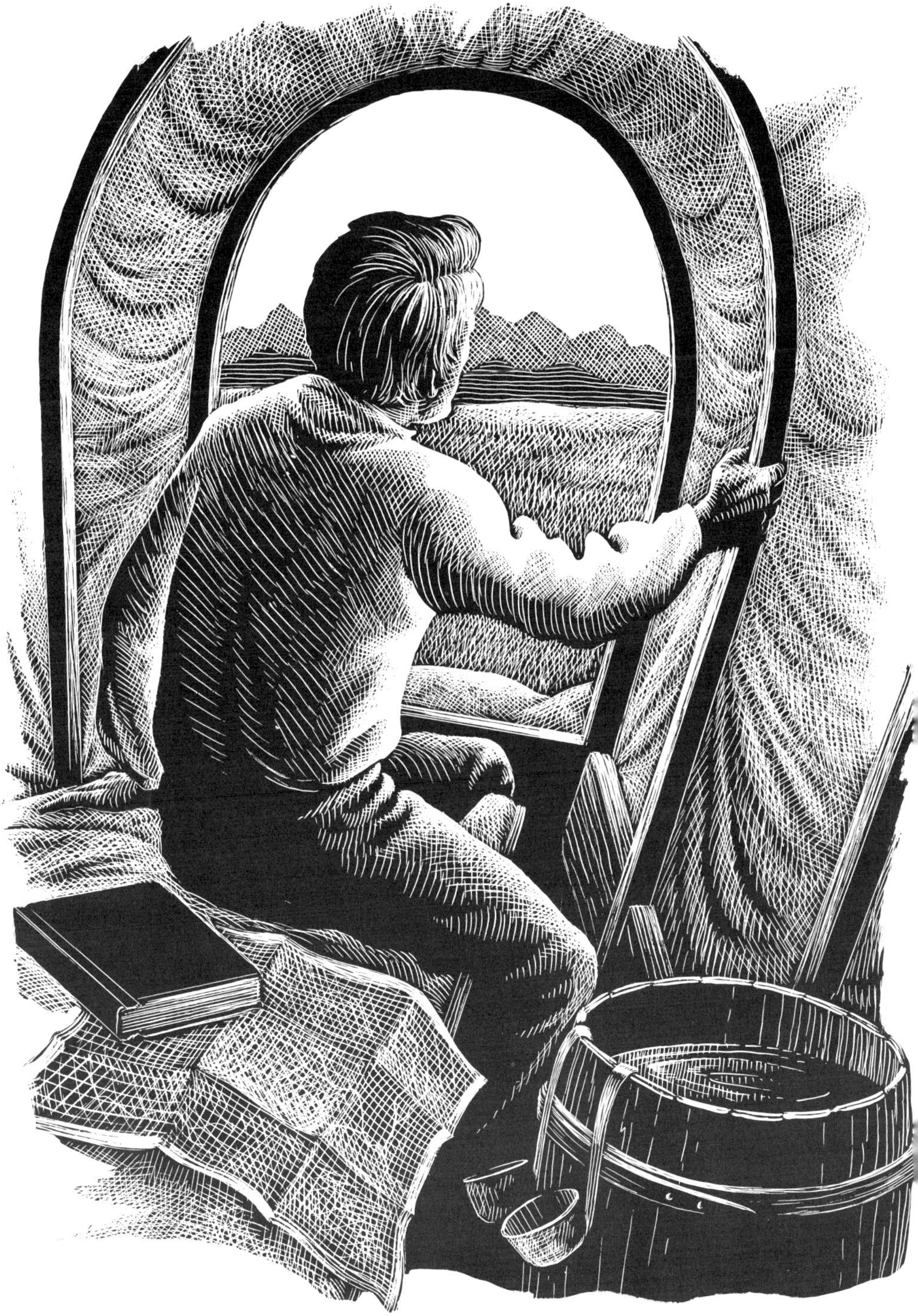

a lively tune as the women and children and men who had not been able to make the long march with the Mormon Battalion tumbled out of their wagons for a first look at the Valley. With them was a company of Mormons who had come all the way from Mississippi.

Sam Brannon, who had ridden in with the Pueblo Saints and the Mississippi Company, looked out over the drab valley to the Great Salt Lake. He thought that the Salt Lake Valley was a miserable place compared with beautiful California.

"Shall I lead my people already well settled on good farming land or busy at their trades back to this desolate place?" he asked Brigham Young.

Brigham Young answered, "The Saints who came on the *Brooklyn* and the Battalion men that are in California should stay where they are at least until next year. They should work through the winter and bring their earnings back to the Valley."

Sam Brannon turned on his heel and walked away so that Brigham Young couldn't see the anger in his flashing black eyes. When the anger had cooled he left the Valley for the long trip back to San Francisco Bay. The eagerness had gone from his face, the energy from his voice. But with Sam Brannon discouragement did not last long. "We will build a beautiful city," he said. "We will find hidden wealth that will bring the world flocking to our doors."

He did not know then that his own newspaper, *The California Star*, would send the news of the gold strike in California to every part of the country and start the gold rush of '49. He did not know that he would be California's first millionaire; that he would build railroads and finance banks. He didn't know that he would be the most important man in California to bring law and order and sound government to the wild and ruthless West.

Brigham Young knew that a land as beautiful as the California Sam Brannon had described would soon be overrun with men wanting to make quick fortunes—men like the neighbors who had driven the Saints out of Ohio and Missouri and Illinois.

Brigham Young looked at the desert stretching away to the salt sea and said, "We will work hard. We will pray as if God were going to do everything for us. Then we will work as hard as if we were going to have to do everything for ourselves. We will make this desert blossom as the rose."

MILLIONS OF CRICKETS

When the Mormons had been in the Valley less than a week everybody had been put to work. Surveying instruments were taken from one of the wagons and a surveyor, a rodman and a chainman were busy laying out a city in square blocks just as Nauvoo had been laid out. A site for a temple was chosen and surveyed.

Hunters brought in meat for all of the men, women and children. Some of the men went into the mountains to cut wood; others hauled the wood in to the new settlement. Some went on with the plowing and planting. No one was too young to do a share. The children picked up the rocks that were turned over by the plows and carried them to the edge of the fields.

Everybody who was not working at something else helped to build a stockade. "All of the Indians are not friendly," Brigham Young said. "We must have some protection for the women and children." The walls were to be twenty-seven inches thick and nine feet high. This wall would be the outside wall of the houses that faced the square. There would be heavy gates at the east and west ends of the fort. In the center of the open square the men planted a flag pole. The Stars and Stripes waved in the breeze. On another pole hung the bell which had once hung in the Nauvoo Temple. It was rung to call the people to morning and evening prayer.

One day Brigham Young called John Smith to his side. "I am going to leave you in charge of the Saints here in the Valley. I want you to see that all of the buildings we have planned are finished. I want you to see that the crops are carefully harvested. We must always remember that more and more Saints are moving toward us over the westward trail."

"But where will you be?" John Smith asked Brigham Young.

"I will be busy. Do not worry about that. I and Heber Kimball and a few other men will return to Winter Quarters."

"Return to Winter Quarters! Why you have just got here."

"The Saints in Winter Quarters will need help to get ready to finish their journey. You can take care of things here." Then Brigham Young's voice grew very low. "You may all be hungry. Do not let the people eat their seed. That must be saved for another planting."

On August second Brigham Young called a meeting in the bowery. "Who will be willing to go with me back to Winter Quarters?" he asked. Nearly every man raised his hand.

As Brigham Young and his party traveled back toward Winter Quarters they met several westbound companies. Altogether fifteen hundred men, women and children with five hundred and sixty wagons and five thousand head of stock were on their way to the Valley. At the Sweetwater, Brigham Young and his party met two companies moving west. They stopped over a day and had a big party. The women unpacked their dishes and prepared a fine dinner. Everybody sang and danced and told stories through the afternoon and evening.

On the first of November Brigham Young and his party entered Winter Quarters. There would be much to do there before it was travel time again. "We will take care of the poor," Brigham Young said. "We will watch over the widows and the orphans. We will give them first place because their need is greatest."

After Brigham Young left the Salt Lake Valley all of the men and women did their best to follow his instructions. Meat was scarce, there was little butter, not much milk. Sometimes the hunters brought in wild meat. The people learned to eat the bulb of the wild sego lily and wild parsnip roots. There were many mouths to be fed. Twenty-one hundred people arrived in the Valley during that first summer and autumn.

Clothing was scarce. Very few people had shoes, though some had moccasins made from elk or deer skin. One man cut the hair from his curly dog and his wife made the hair into a suit of clothes, spinning and weaving the hair herself. Women even learned to spin cow and buffalo hair as well as wool.

People lived through the winter, singing, dancing, and praying as well as working. They were glad when spring came and new crops could be planted.

Brigham Young had told the men to fence the fields so that the stock would not spoil the new growing wheat. "I would rather have a ten-acre field fenced, than one hundred acres plowed, planted and left to the cattle," he said.

But in the early summer of 1848, just as the heads were beginning to form on the wheat the sky was blackened by swarms of crickets. The crickets came down upon the new fields and began to eat off every blade of grass. They bit off the tops of the wheat then ate the heads. Men, women and children tried to fight the crickets. The men made big paddles and set the boys to beating the crickets into the irrigation ditches with the hope that they would be drowned. Others set fires hoping to burn them. In many fields two boys stretched a long rope and walked back and forth trying to knock the crickets off the yellowing heads.

At last the people said, "We can do nothing. This is the end for us. We are twelve hundred miles from any markets. Soon countless thousands will come from the East across the plains to join us in our starvation."

John Smith called the people to come to the bowery. "We will go without food for three days. And while we fast we will pray. Jesus has said, 'Ask and ye shall receive.' We can do nothing more for ourselves."

So the Mormons fasted for three days. They prayed. They watched the crickets moving on across their fields.

Suddenly, from the west came hundreds of snow-white gulls. They, too, settled upon the fields. "What now?" the people cried. "These birds will eat all of the grain that is left."

"Look," someone cried. "The birds are not eating the grain, they are eating the crickets!"

The gulls swallowed the crickets, then when their crops were full they hopped over to a ditch or a convenient hill and vomited the crickets out. Then they ate some more.

All that Sunday the people went about in thankful

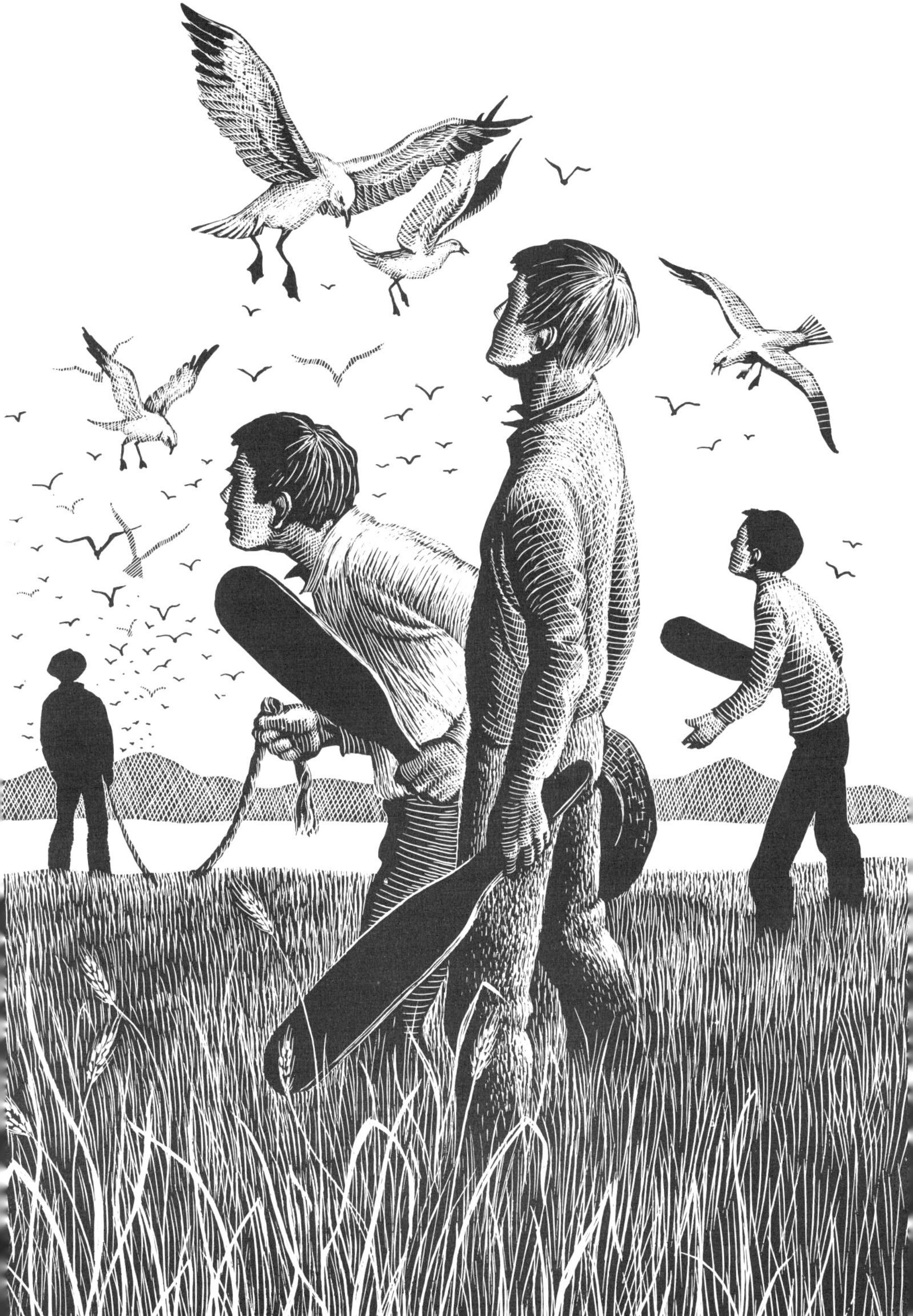

prayer, and the next day they found the edges of their water ditches piled high with dead crickets. The gulls, who had flown away in the evening, came like a cloud the next morning.

Brigham Young, away at Winter Quarters, did not know of the miracle that had saved his people. But the people did not forget.

In Utah no one may kill a gull, and in the spring a plume of gulls follows each plowman. There is a monument built to the gulls, too, a beautiful column with a group of fluttering gulls at its tip. To this day the Mormon boys and girls hear the story of the crickets and the gulls and feel thankful that those first pioneers did not starve to death in the wilderness.

HANDCART PIONEERS

Brigham Young sat in his office with two of his counselors. He was reading a letter he had just received from England. When he had finished he looked up and said, "Many penniless people in England want to come to this Valley."

Brigham Young and his counselors could look out of the windows. They could see the neat houses of log or sundried brick surrounded by gardens and young orchards. Outside of the city the green fields stretched out toward the mountains. They could see the wide streets. The pioneers had been in the Valley only eight years but water from the mountain streams now ran between grassy banks in every part of the little city. Green trees shaded the sidewalks between the irrigation ditches and the neat picket fences. To those four men who had worked so hard to build it, Salt Lake City looked very beautiful.

"We have room and to spare for the English Saints," one of the men said.

"There is room here, yes, but these Saints do not have the money to bring themselves here. This letter is from Franklin D. Richards. He says that most of the Saints who could pay their passage and outfit themselves to cross the plains have already left. There are many in England who work in the mines and the mills and who have never made more than enough to barely live on. Some of the miners go to work before sunup and stay in the mines under the ground until sundown in the evening. They never see the light of day."

"Here the men and women could work in the fields and gardens. We must help them to come to Salt Lake City," one of the counselors said.

But another asked, "How can they come if they have no money? They cannot sail on the ships without money. They cannot ride on the train without money. They cannot buy wagons and oxen and mules and supplies for the long trip across the plains without money."

Brigham Young said, "These men are our brothers. We must help them. We will pay for their passage on the ship. We will pay for them to ride the train to the end of the line at Iowa City. But we cannot buy wagons and oxen and mules for them." Then he was silent for a long time.

"I have an idea. I know of young men coming on foot with their knapsacks on their backs who are going to California to find gold. If a man would do that for gold why wouldn't he do it for God?"

The counselors didn't answer. They watched Brigham Young's face.

"We could have handcarts built to carry each pioneer's supplies. Those who want to come to the Valley could walk, pushing and pulling these handcarts."

"Walk!" his counselors said. "Walk a thousand miles?"

"More than a thousand miles. Fourteen hundred miles," Brigham Young said. "But that is not impossible. Every man who has driven an ox team across the plains has walked by the animals. Much time is lost when oxen stray away and pioneers have to stop to look for them. Yes, we will prepare a cart for each family. The family can put its own blankets and cooking utensils in the carts. We will send a few wagons to haul the heavy supplies. We will furnish milk cows so the children can have milk; and beef cattle so that the people will have meat."

Brigham Young wrote a letter to Franklin Richards telling about the plan; the men and women were happy. "We will walk. We will be happy to push a handcart." Many of these men and women had never been outside their own little village. They had never built a campfire nor slept out under the stars. They did not know what was before them.

Franklin Richards arranged for two ships, the *Thornton*

and the *Horizon*. These ships would bring the Saints to New York. More than sixteen hundred men, women and children crowded on to these two ships. They were as happy as if they were going on a picnic. Some of them had musical instruments. They played their instruments and the music cheered everybody.

When the ships arrived in New York the band played again. Everybody tumbled out of the ships and into the trains. The first company arrived in Iowa City late in June.

Brigham Young had sent some experienced men to help the English Saints get started on their long walk. These men were surprised to see so many people! They had expected only half this many. More handcarts had to be built, more tents had to be sewed. More cattle and cows had to be purchased. More ox-drawn wagons would be needed.

Everybody worked to help the impatient Saints get on their way.

The carts were made as wide as the covered wagons so that the wheels could roll in the ruts made by the wagon wheels. They were made of hickory or oak. Even the oak carts had hickory axles so that the carts would not break down on the trail. The shafts were five to six feet long. There were crossbars nailed from one shaft to the other so that the man or woman or boy could lean against the bar when he pulled the cart.

These Saints from England had never been out in the open country before. They were pale, and thin. They laughed and sang and felt as if they were on a long, wonderful holiday.

When the carts were finished the company started out.

First went the older people and the children who would not be able to push the heavy carts, next came the mile-long line of carts, then the supply wagons.

The hot Iowa sun beat down upon them as they walked. They were not prepared for the sunburn, the heat rash, the discomfort. No one had told them about the insects that would bite them.

When the heat wave finally broke, the rain came with such a rush of thunder, lightning and wind that they thought the end of the world was near. Some tried to keep the tents from blowing away, others tried to rescue their little treasures hidden away in the carts. The storm was over as suddenly as it had begun and the Saints dried out as they walked along. They sang:

> *For some must push and some must pull*
> *As we go marching up the hill,*
> *As merrily on the way we go*
> *Until we reach the Valley, oh!*

In the evenings, after supper around the camp fires, the people who had been walking all day danced to the music of the band. On Sunday they did not travel at all, but stayed in camp and held church services, singing and praying and listening to the words of their leaders.

As they crossed Iowa several children died. These were poorly fed, frail children who might have died if they had stayed at home in the dark factory or mining towns of Wales and England. The parents knew that folks died even when they traveled by ox-cart; but they grieved as they pushed along the trail away from the little graves.

The Saints and their handcarts were ferried across the

Missouri River to Winter Quarters. Here they stayed for ten days mending their handcarts which had already begun to break down though they had traveled only three hundred miles.

The next thousand miles seemed much more than three times as long as the trip across Iowa. Folks still sang. Many of them felt better than they ever had in their lives. They were burned to a healthy tan. Going barefooted, their feet had become hardened to the trail. There was not enough food and everybody was hungry—but still everybody was happy.

"You must not kill the buffalo even when you are

hungry," their leaders told them. "The buffalo are the Indians' cattle. The Indians will be angry if we kill them."

So the Saints paid the Indians for killing buffalo for them whenever they saw Indians and buffalo at the same time. The Mormons carried tobacco to use for medicine for sick cattle and oxen. The Indians would kill a buffalo for a few cents worth of tobacco.

The company passed Scotts Bluff, Fort Laramie and came to the last crossing of the Platte River.

"Why does our leader make us walk so fast?" they asked. "Why does he push us to walk twenty-six miles in one day when a wagon train travels only ten?"

No one had an answer for these questions. No one but their leader. He knew that the supplies were very, very low. He wanted them to reach Fort Bridger before the food gave out completely. At Fort Bridger Brigham Young would have more supplies waiting for them.

Three months from the time they had left Iowa City the handcart pioneers broke out of the mouth of Emigration Canyon where nine years before Brigham Young had said, "This is the place."

Half the people of Salt Lake City were there to greet them. There was Brigham Young, and Heber Kimball, and Pitt's Brass Band.

Tired as they were, many of the people who had pushed or pulled a handcart for 1400 miles danced a jig because they were so happy. Some cried because the joy was too much to stand. All of the handcart pioneers were invited to the homes of the Mormons. Again they slept in real beds. Again they ate food at real tables.

"Why didn't you write letters to us to tell how you were getting along?" the Saints in Salt Lake City asked the handcart pioneers.

"There was no wagon train, no mule train, not even a single horseman passed us." The handcart company had been the fastest thing on the road!

Two weeks after the first two companies left Iowa City a third party took out after them. This party was made up of Mormons from Wales, and these folks, even the very old and the very young, were good walkers. One woman of seventy-three walked every step of the way. They walked more than twenty miles a day and came into Salt Lake Valley just a week behind the first two companies. Again the town turned out and Pitt's band played the handcart pioneers into town.

"The handcart idea was a fine one," Brigham Young said happily. "We can bring over many Saints who are too poor to outfit themselves with oxen, mules and wagons."

Later that summer two more companies got off the train at Iowa City. It was July, much later than any handcart pioneers had been expected. There were no handcarts built and there was no seasoned lumber to build them. "A thousand people. What will we ever do!" the men that Brigham Young had sent to Iowa City to help the earlier companies said.

"We must build carts out of any wood we can get," another said.

So they set to work and built 260 carts. The women sewed tents and the men who could not build carts found cattle and cows to buy. They bought wagons and filled them with provisions.

Finally, the middle of July, five hundred men, women and children, the Willie Company, started out with the hastily built carts. By the end of the month another five hundred, the Martin Company, was on the trail.

Crossing Iowa the companies made good time, but when they got to Winter Quarters some of them knew that winter was not far away. "Shall we go on? Shall we stay here until next spring?" they asked each other. Brother Richards, who was traveling in a small fast company of mule-drawn wagons, loved these brave people. "If you will stay I will hurry on and tell Brigham Young to provide you

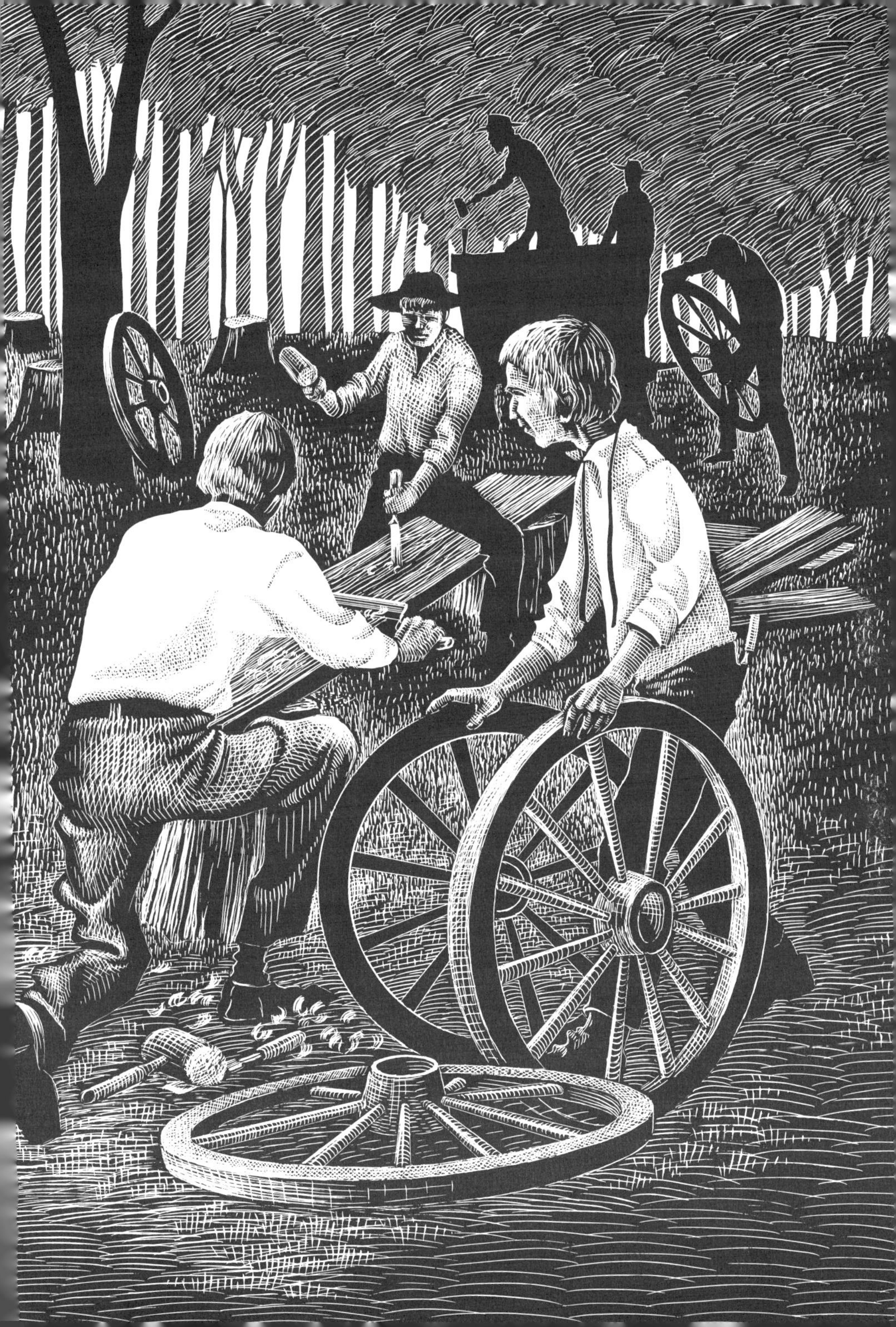

with supplies for the winter. If you feel you must come, may the Lord be with you."

"Oh, let's try it," most of the Saints said. So they started out hoping that winter would come late. On each cart an extra hundred pounds of flour was placed.

The people pushed on bravely, but when they reached the far west the green wood in their carts began to warp and their carts fell to pieces. People went without bacon to eat so that they could grease axles with the bacon and keep the cart wheels turning. When the carts broke down they stopped to fix them, then hurried on to make up the time.

One night a group of Indians drove off the cows, the beef cattle and the oxen that pulled the supply wagons. The drivers searched and searched but they lost thirty animals. Another time a herd of buffalo swept down upon the straggling pioneers. Some found shelter under their carts as they watched the herd thunder by. More of the beef cattle and cows went off with the buffalo.

It was September before these companies reached Fort Laramie. There were still five hundred miles to go, and winter could come any day. Captain Willie cut flour rations to three-fourths of a pound a day. Everybody was hungry. Everybody was weak, but they pushed on, still singing:

For some must push and some must pull
As we go marching up the hill.

Nights were cold and many of the people had thrown away blankets to make their loads lighter. In October the weary marchers felt snow on their faces. They should hurry to reach Salt Lake City before winter came. But no one could hurry. The long line of pioneers plodded on, thinking only of lifting each foot to take another step forward. No one sang any more. There was no energy to sing. Even when camp was broken each morning and the dead were buried in snow banks because the ground was frozen hard, no one sang:

And should we die before our journey's through,
Happy day, all is well;
We then are free from toil and trial, too.
With the just we shall dwell.

Finally when there was no food left and no one had the energy to take another step, the company camped in some willows. People were so tired and hungry they went to sleep and didn't wake up again.

Several days' travel behind them the Martin handcart company camped on the banks of the Platte. Winter had come and they couldn't move in the face of a storm. When the snow stopped they dragged themselves a few more miles.

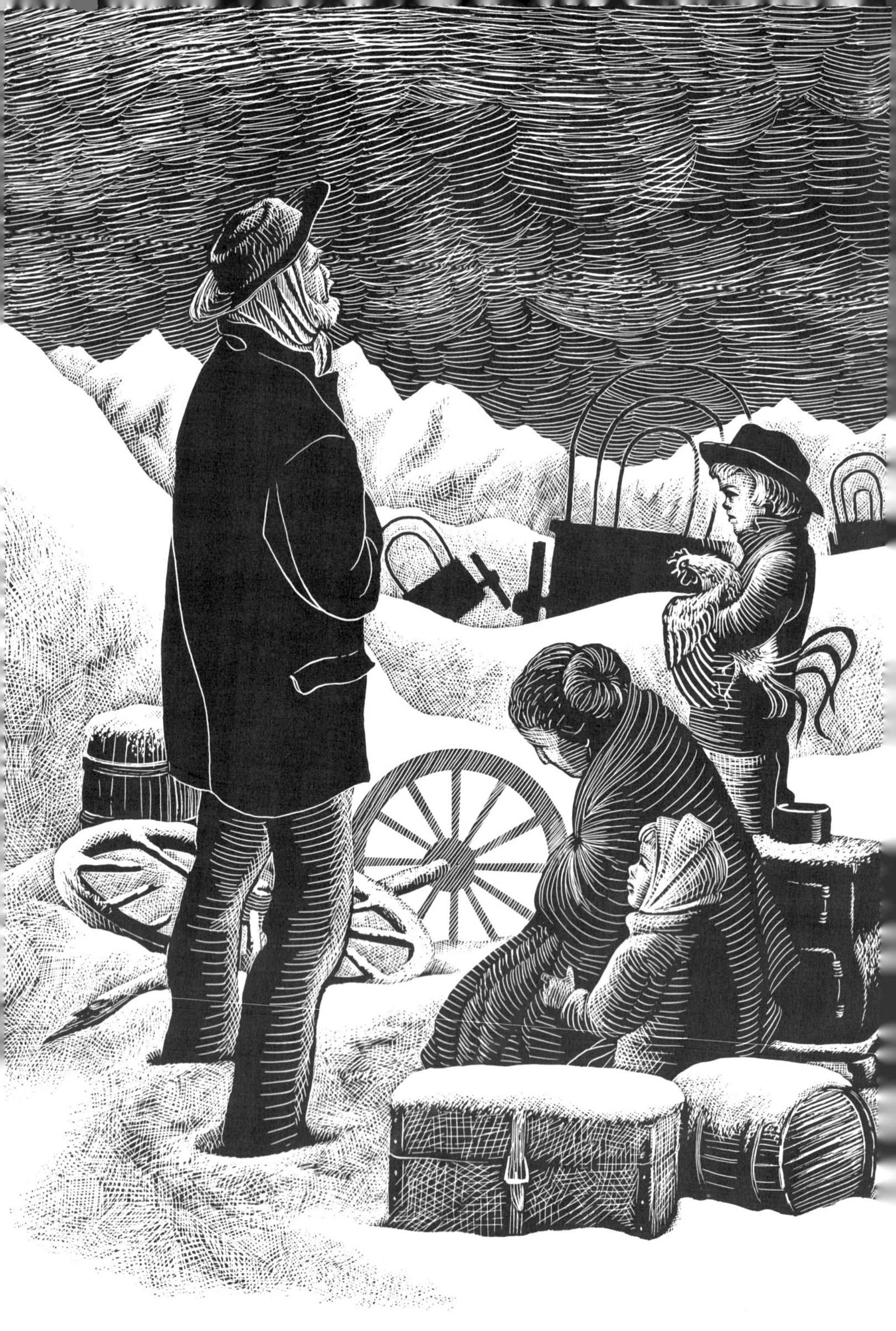

Again a three-day snow caught them. There was nothing to do but to stop and wait for death to overtake them.

In Salt Lake City the Mormons were having a conference. Brother Richards told Brigham Young about the Willie Company and the Martin Company who had pushed on westward even though the season was late. Two other travelers had passed the Willie and the Martin companies. They told Brigham Young that the snow had already fallen and that the people could not reach the Salt Lake Valley before winter caught them.

"We will not sit here and talk," Brigham Young said. "They are our brothers. We must help them."

With his own money he outfitted some wagons with strong, fast teams. Heber Kimball outfitted some wagons, too. Brigham Young said, "If anybody else wants to volunteer his wagon to take it out to bring these poor people into the Valley let him do it."

All the women began gathering warm clothing and blankets and quilts. The men were busy putting flour and other provisions into the wagons. The people asked each other, "Will these handcart pioneers live until we reach them with supplies?"

Eph Hanks, a powerful young man, with another scout rode out in front of the wagon train. He had passed these people when he was taking mail to the East and again when he was bringing mail back from St. Louis. Would he find the freezing, starving Saints just outside Salt Lake City in Echo Canyon? He hallowed but the rocks gave back his voice. Would he find them on the plains of Wyoming? The plains were a sheet of snow as far as he could see. Would he find them at Fort Bridger? A snowstorm came out of the north, but still Eph pushed on. The handcart pioneers were not at Fort Bridger.

On he went, digging the ice from the nostrils of his horse so that the animal could breathe. Suddenly out of the cold and snow came a great buffalo. As many times as Eph had crossed this way in carrying the mail he had never seen a buffalo in this part of Wyoming. He raised his musket and with one shot killed the animal. There in the freezing weather he dressed it and hung the meat over his tired horse. Walking and leading the horse, bent under the load of the buffalo meat, he came at last upon the Willie party. The Willie party was no longer a company. The people and the carts were scattered way back along the trail.

Eph built fires to cook the meat. He told the folks, "The supply trains are behind me. Have faith and hold out until they come. Another day and the wagons filled with food and clothing and warm blankets will be here."

Then he mounted his tired horse and went to carry hope to the Martin Company, strung out along the trail still farther from food and shelter.

Half the rescue wagons stayed to help the Willie Company. Half went on to help the Martin Company camped between the Sweetwater and Red Butte.

Not one of the Martin Company expected to live to see Salt Lake Valley. To lighten their loads they had thrown away too much. Some didn't even have a blanket to cover them. They had nothing to eat but the oxen who had starved to death on the snow-covered plain.

The coming of the rescue wagons was not an end to suffering and trouble. There were still three hundred miles to go. Some of the pioneers traveled on pushing their handcarts after they had been given food and clothing. Some rode in the rescue wagons. Some of them—with the end of the journey in sight—died. One girl died while she was lifting a cracker to her lips.

The first rescue wagon entered the valley on November the ninth. One woman stood up in the wagon and cried, "Thank God, I again see the land of the living!"

Day after day others struggled in. The Saints took these worn-out pioneers into their homes and fed them, cared for them, nursed them back to health.

Still each day brought its stragglers. A young girl put everything she owned into her handcart then, with a mighty push, she sent the whole thing crashing down into a ravine. "I've had enough of handcarts," she cried.

But the Mormons in England had not had enough of handcarts. Leaving early enough to make the trip before autumn, two companies came in 1857, one in 1859 and two in 1860.

These pale, thin miners and factory workers from England didn't look like the toughest, bravest men in America. But they were.

For some must push and some must pull
As we go marching up the hill,
As merrily on the way we go
Until we reach the Valley, oh!

THE IRON HORSE

Twenty years after Brigham Young had first seen the Salt Lake Valley stretching out to the great salt sea and had said, "This is the place," 90,000 people lived in this isolated land. Villages were cupped in the high mountain valleys, towns squatted on the fertile land that sloped gently toward the Great Salt Lake and Utah Lake, the fresh water lake that lay to the south. The villages were like bright beads on a green ribbon stretching from Salt Lake City in to Idaho and Wyoming on the north and in to Nevada and Arizona on the south.

Every one of the 90,000 people, except those who had been born in this pioneer land, had made a long and difficult journey to get there.

The Mormons had reached the settled frontier in several ways. Many of those who had come from northern Europe and England, Scotland and Wales had taken ship to New Orleans. There they had transferred to a river steamer and chugged up the Mississippi River to St. Louis. At St. Louis they had changed to a smaller river boat and traveled slowly up the Missouri River to an outfitting station in Iowa—perhaps Kanesville or Council Bluffs.

Other European Saints had landed in New York and crowded into passenger and freight cars and come by rail to Iowa City, the western terminus of the railroad.

Many Mormons who lived near the Atlantic Ocean had gone by boat to the Isthmus of Panama, crossed the Isthmus, and taken another boat up the Pacific Coast. Still others had followed the course of the Good Ship *Brooklyn* and gone all the way around the Horn.

No matter how the trip was begun, it ended with a long, long journey by covered wagon or by handcart.

Now that the desert had really started to "blossom as the rose," thousands more wanted to join Brigham Young and the Mormons. For them the journey would be quicker and easier. Already the "Iron Horse" had begun to puff its way across the continent.

Just seven years after the first company of Saints had arrived in the Valley, Theodore Judah, a twenty-eight-year-old engineer who had never even heard of the Mormons, was invited to build a railroad from Sacramento into the rich mining country. Judah quickly built the road to Folsom, twenty-two miles from Sacramento. There the company ran out of money. This twenty-two miles of rail was the only railroad in all of California.

Judah had such big dreams that people called him *Crazy Judah*. He could see in his imagination railroad tracks binding the Atlantic to the Pacific.

Judah said, "If the western states are to be a part of the great United States there must be a railroad!"

Since there was no money to build the railroad farther than Folsom, Judah hurried away to Washington. Here he tried to interest everybody in passing a law that would help to build the railroad. At that time Congress could think of nothing but the question of slavery. No one had time to listen to *Crazy Judah*. He was not discouraged. He went back to California.

In Sacramento he got a job surveying a road through the Sierra mountains for a wagon company that wanted to freight goods to the new mines in Nevada. He surveyed the wagon road just as he had been hired to do, but on his own time he selected a possible route for a railroad to get through the mountains.

At Dutch Flat, on the counter of a drugstore, he drew up *Articles of Association of the Central Pacific Railroad of California*.

Now he hurried back to San Francisco. Judah was always hurrying.

"We must build a railroad," he told the businessmen of San Francisco.

"Build a railroad through the mountains?" they laughed. "Why, man, are you crazy? The snow is thirty feet deep there in the winter time."

So the young engineer with the crazy dream went back to Sacramento. He wasn't ready to give up yet. In Sacramento he talked with a Mr. Bailey who showed some interest. Mr. Bailey said he had a merchant friend, Leland Stanford, who might be interested, also. *Crazy Judah* called a meeting of the businessmen who were interested. They were Leland Stanford, his partner Collis P. Huntington and Charlie Crocker.

"If you want to get control of the rich new mining towns in Nevada," he told them, "you will need a railroad to freight in supplies to them and to bring out the ore."

The small town merchants saw sense in what Judah said.

Theodore hurried back to Washington. He told of the wonders of the West and urged people to think of the United States as a nation that stretched from coast to coast. He talked with congressmen and senators and in 1862 Congress passed a law that would make a railroad across the continent a possibility. Congress said that ten alternate sections out of each mile of land belonging to the government should go to the builders of the railroad. This land was to be on both sides of the line as far as the tracks ran. It agreed to lend money in addition to giving the land, but no money was to be loaned until forty miles of track were completed.

Theodore hurried back to Sacramento to begin the building. A great celebration was held in Sacramento the day that the ground was broken to begin the grading for the tracks. The day was January 8, 1863. A band played and frock-coated speakers climbed to a platform to give long speeches. The January rains had just begun and the people who had come to hear the band and the speakers moved about in a sea of mud. Bales of hay were brought for them to stand on while they listened. Some thought that the rainy day of the ground-breaking meant that the road would meet with disaster, but Judah, the dreamer, was happy.

He began the building of the road. Almost at once he found that his four friends, Stanford, Huntington, Crocker and Bailey could never share his dream.

"We must build this forty miles of road as cheaply as we can," the four men said.

"We must not even think of expense," Judah said,

"We must put in only the best material. We must build it as well as we can."

"We must build cheaply and quickly so that we can begin to get government help," they insisted.

Judah quarreled with them and started back to New York. Some say he intended to raise money in the East and buy out the four Sacramento businessmen. On the way back he got yellow fever and didn't live to reach New York. Someone else would have to see his dream come true.

The Big Four, as Stanford, Huntington, Crocker and Bailey were called, didn't find railroad building easy. Every workingman in California was interested in mining. The Big Four offered to take men free of charge from San Francisco and Sacramento to the point where the railroad was being built. Two thousand laborers were taken to one point and only one hundred went to work on the railroad. The others gladly accepted the free transportation and then hurried away to the mines. Even those who went to work did not stay long. As soon as they had enough money to start mining they left their work.

"We must employ Chinese workmen," Charlie Crocker said.

"Chinese!" the others objected. "It takes strong men

to grade for the railroad, to blast out tunnels and to build bridges. The Chinese are little people. They don't weigh more than a hundred pounds apiece."

"Look," Charlie Crocker said in his noisy, jovial way, "any race that can build the great wall of China can build a railroad."

"We can try," the others agreed doubtfully.

The first fifty Chinese workmen that were sent to the end of the line made a clean camp quickly, ate a supper of rice and fell to sleep at once without quarreling. The next morning they were up with the sun and ready to work. The little blue-clad men with their pigtails and basket hats swarmed like bees over the work to be done and did it with quietness and efficiency. "Give me more Chinese!" Charlie Crocker roared.

Soon the Big Four were importing Chinese laborers from across the Pacific. Before the railroad was completed almost a thousand men had been brought from China.

The problem of workmen wasn't the only thing that worried the Big Four. Every foot of rail had to be brought by ship all the way around the Horn. It took eight to ten months to make the trip so there was delay after delay in obtaining the material. The material was costly, too. The freight charge on one locomotive was $8,100. Twenty engines cost $400,000.

The men in San Francisco who said that Judah was crazy to think of building a railroad through the Sierras had been right about the weather. The snow *was* thirty feet deep and more. At least four times an avalanche swept a camp away. Buildings, supplies, men were all buried deep in a canyon not to be found until spring.

Slowly, almost inch by inch, the Central Pacific Railroad Company pushed its tracks toward the Nevada-California line.

While the Central Pacific Railroad was pushing across the Sierra Mountains, another railroad was building west from Omaha.

Men who had thought that a railroad could follow the trail west made by Brigham Young and his pioneers—the trail along the Platte River and through the Rocky Mountains—had been talking with congressmen in Washington just as Judah had. The Railroad Act which Abraham Lincoln signed into law in 1862 not only gave the Central Pacific Company the right to build from the west to the east, but gave the Union Pacific Company the right to build from the east to the west. The Act chartered a company to be known as the Union Pacific Railway Company.

But in those Civil War days money was hard to get and the Union Pacific Company didn't start to build its railroad until the autumn of 1865.

Rafts on the Mississippi carried the ties and bridge

timbers from the North. Steamboats and barges brought the steel from St. Joseph, Missouri. Ox teams brought other material from Chicago and Iowa City.

The Pacific Railroad had had to fight the cold, long winter and the deep snows and sudden blizzards. The Union Pacific had to fight the Indians.

In spite of the Indian trouble the road seemed to shoot forward. A writer whose name we don't know says this is the way the line was laid.

> "*A light car drawn by a single horse gallops up to the front with its load of rails. Two men seize the end of a rail and start forward, the rest of the gang taking hold by two until it is clear of the car. They come forward at a run. At the word of command the rail is dropped in its place, right side up with care, while the same process goes on at the other side of the car. Less than thirty seconds to a rail for each gang so four rails go down to the minute. The moment the car is emptied it is tipped over on the side of the track to let the next loaded car pass it, and then it is tipped back again. It is a sight to see it go flying back for another load, propelled by a horse at full gallop at the end of 60 or 80 feet of rope, ridden by a young Jehu, who drives furiously. Close behind the first gang come the gaugers, spiker and bolters, and a lively time they make of it. It is a grand anvil chorus that those sturdy sledges are playing across the plains. There are 10 spikes to a rail, 400 rails to a mile, 1800 miles to San Francisco. 21,000,000 times those sledges to be slung.*"

When the Central Pacific had crossed the California-Nevada line, the Union Pacific that had started building

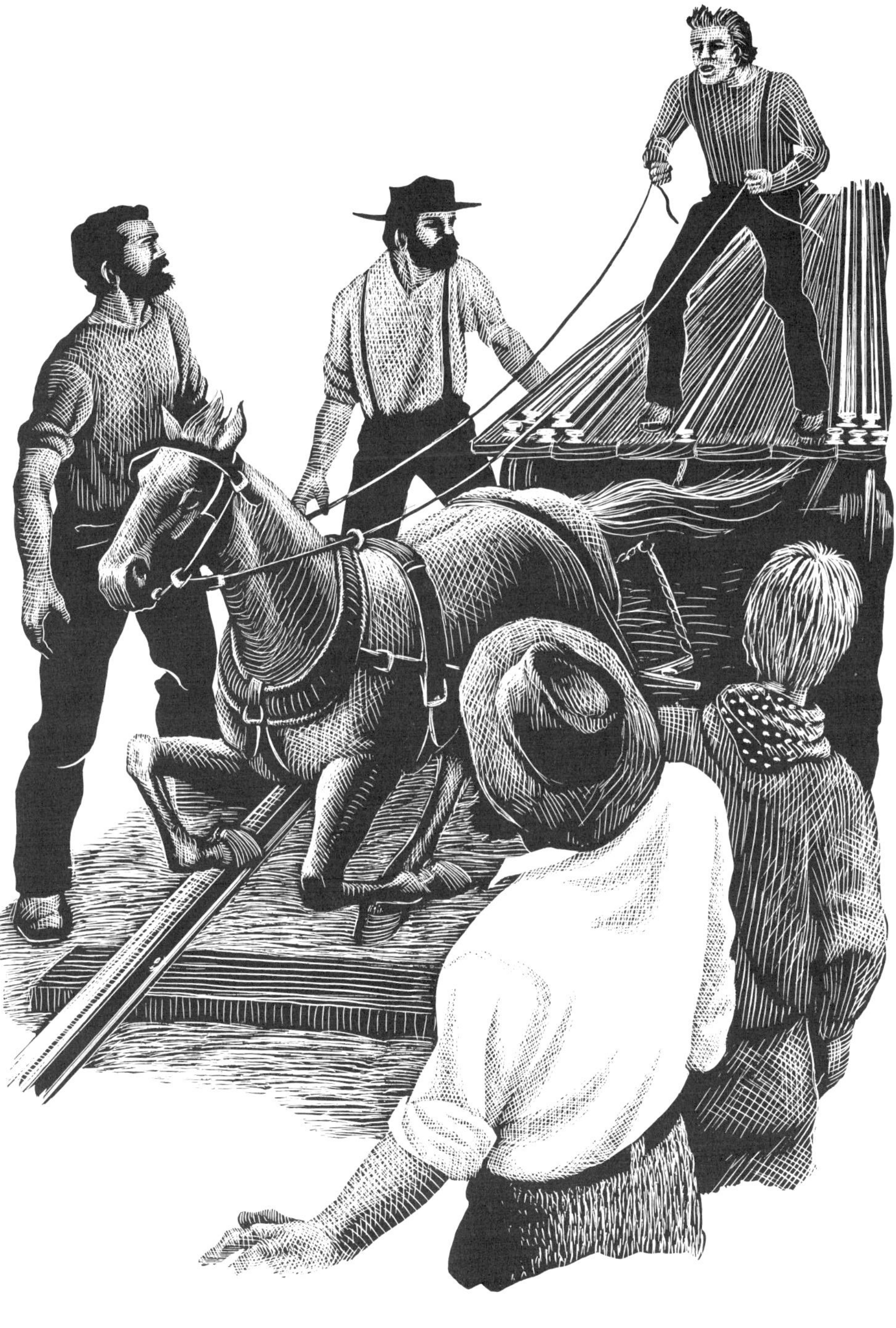

so much later was already crossing the Rocky Mountains and was in Wyoming.

Now the greatest race in history was on.

"We must push our line through Utah," the Big Four said. "We must have the government land and the government bonds."

"We must push our way through Utah," General Dodge said. "The Union Pacific must have all that government land and those government bonds."

The Central Pacific sent railroad graders eighty miles east of Ogden, Utah. The Union Pacific sent surveyors and graders as far west as Humboldt Wells, Nevada.

Now the two companies had men working almost within shouting distance of each other.

During all of this time Brigham Young and the Mormons did not sit quietly by. They were eager to have the railroad to bring more Mormons to Utah. The Mormons loaned money for the first survey of the land that the Union Pacific tracks would cross.

Brigham Young wanted the railroad but he didn't want the rough railroad workers shooting up the quiet towns. He didn't want the lawless gamblers and the sellers of whiskey to set up shop in the sober farming villages.

In the spring of 1868 Samuel Reed of the Union

Pacific made a contract with Brigham Young. The Mormons were to do the grading and tunneling and bridge work from Echo Canyon in the Rocky Mountains to the shores of Great Salt Lake. Five thousand men were to work at two dollars a day.

"We will bring any Mormon now in the East out to the end of our lines," Mr. Reed said. "Any man who wants to work on our railroad can travel free, and his wife and children can come at a reduced fare."

"This will open up the way for many poor immigrants," Brigham Young said. "We will accept your offer."

Very soon Leland Stanford of the Central Pacific asked Brigham Young to build the road from Humboldt Wells in Nevada to Ogden, Utah. Brigham Young agreed, so the Mormons were working on both roads.

In May 1869 the road was finished. The two companies agreed to join the Central Pacific tracks and the Union Pacific tracks at Promontory Point on the north end of the Great Salt Lake.

Five or six hundred people came on the trains to watch the driving of the golden spike. Government troops came from Fort Douglas in Salt Lake City. With the troops was the army band. Men in frock coats had prepared long orations for the occasion. Standing about were Mexicans,

105

Chinese, Indians, half-breeds, Negroes, Irishmen, other laborers from all parts of the United States.

The last tie was placed under rails by the construction superintendent of each road. A prayer was offered. The gold spike was put in place. The officials were to drive it in with a sledge hammer. The telegraph was set up to carry the sound of the hammer striking the spike. But the officials were excited. They couldn't seem to hit the spike. They kept hitting the ties instead.

At last the spike was driven and the two engines that stood facing each other were brought up nose to nose. On the Union Pacific side was a new straight stack coal-burning engine. The Central Pacific's locomotive was an older model, a wood burner. The Central Pacific locomotive backed up and the Union Pacific engine ran over the place where the tracks had been joined. Then the Union Pacific engine backed up and the Central Pacific engine ran over the rails that were held by the golden spike.

Now steel rails had girdled the continent. One thousand seven hundred and seventy-five miles of track had been laid. No one would have to take the long journey around the Horn or across the Isthmus of Panama to get to California. No one would have to travel ten miles a day by oxcart to join the Mormons in Salt Lake City.

The steel rails had tied the Valley of the Saints to the West Coast and the East Coast.

Brigham Young's blossoming desert was a part of the great United States.

THE MORMON TRAIL GOES ON

August 29, 1877, a simple message went out over all the telegraph lines of the West:
Brigham Young is dead.
It had been thirty years, one month and five days since Brigham Young had looked over the barren, treeless land that sloped toward the salt-white shore of the Great Salt Lake and had said, "This is the place."

What had happened in the western deserts and the mountain valleys in those thirty years?

From the day that Brigham Young had become the Mormon leader he had had eyes everywhere. He had sent scouts to find the best course for the Mormon Trail. As soon as he had reached the Salt Lake Valley he had sent more scouts to study the land and tell him about it. The scouts told him that the Great Salt Lake was the remnant of what had once been a great inland sea filling the whole valley. Hundreds, or perhaps thousands of years before, the rushing mountain streams, flowing into this great sea, had dropped fertile earth. Now that the lake had grown so much smaller this good land was waiting for the plows and for irriga-

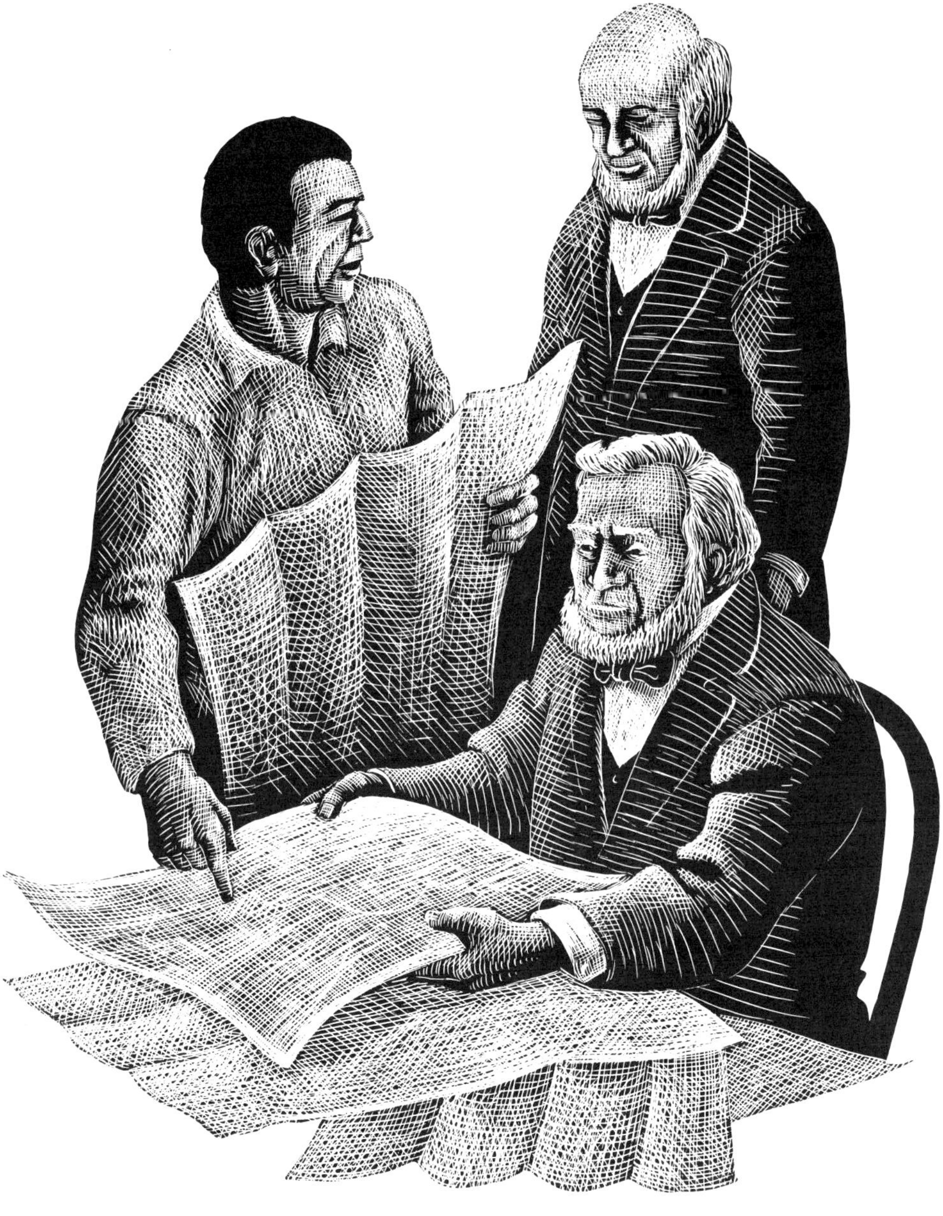

tion water to make it into gardens and orchards. They told him that between the mountain ranges and tucked away in the hills were valleys that could become rich pastures or profitable fields. They even told him about the valleys and streams in Idaho and Nevada, in Colorado and Arizona and California. His scouts told him where the Indians were friendly and where they were warlike. They told him where there were deposits of iron ore and of coal.

As soon as the scouts had made their reports, Brigham Young began to make plans to settle a large part of the West.

The Mormon Trail was like a great rope that led from the Mississippi to the Salt Lake Valley. Now Brigham Young would unravel the western end of that rope and the

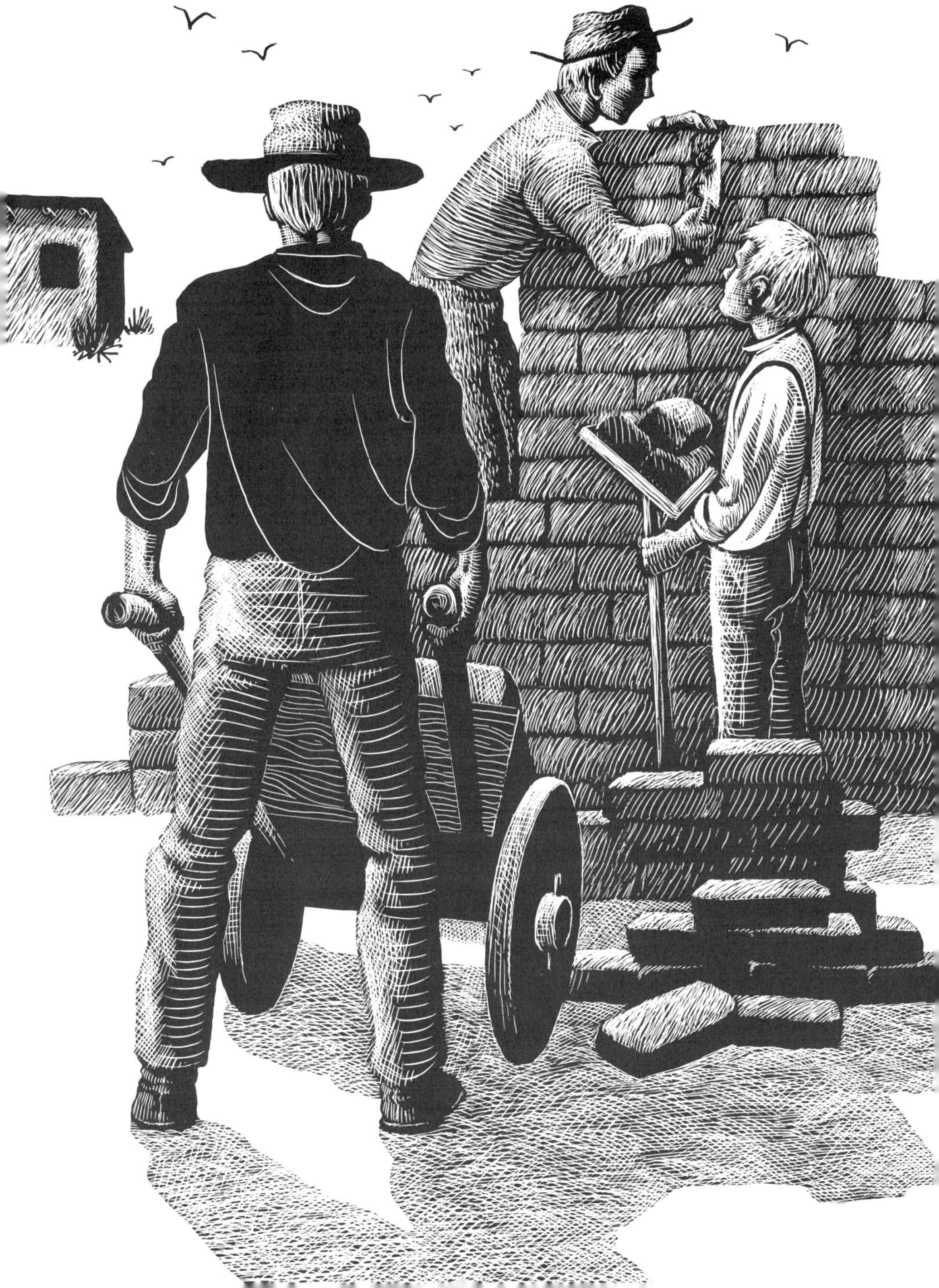

strands would reach almost four hundred miles north to the headwaters of the Salmon River (now in Idaho) and seven hundred and fifty miles southwest to San Bernardino (now in California). Strands would reach into Nevada, Arizona, Wyoming and Colorado. Later a strand would reach south into New Mexico and into Old Mexico and much later north into Canada.

"There are three reasons why we must plant colonies wherever the land will support settlers," Brigham Young told his counselors.

"Salt Lake Valley is already getting crowded?" one of the men guessed.

"That is true," Brigham Young agreed. "But I was not thinking of that. I was thinking that we must take the blessings of the gospel to our red-skinned brothers. They know nothing of Jesus."

"That is the first reason. What is the second?"

"I see hundreds of happy villages surrounded by ripening fields, shaded by quick-growing poplars and box elder trees. Our people will be happy in such villages far away from temptation and troublesome neighbors."

"And third?"

Brigham Young's counselors watched while the whole expression of his face changed.

"Some day," he said, "our state of Deseret will stretch from the Rocky Mountains to the Pacific Ocean. The Saints coming from England will not come by today's route. They will not have to cross all of the states that lie between the Atlantic Ocean and our Valley. I plan to open up a way across the Panama and thus save them 3,000 miles of burdensome travel. We will have a continued line of stations between this valley and the Pacific. We will plant enough colonies so that as night overtakes the traveler he will find the hospitality and protection of one of our settlements."

One of Brigham Young's counselors sighed. "That sounds like a big job, Brother Brigham, for even you to undertake."

Brigham Young smiled. "I am not going to do this alone. One thing that experience and God have taught me is that I must rely on others to carry out these plans. I will divide all of the land that we plan to colonize into large areas. Over each of these areas I will place one or two of you brethren who have proved that you are wise and responsible. Together, with God's help, we will settle the West and build here the Kingdom of God."

As he sat in his office and studied the maps and reports of his scouts, he decided just where he would plant each settlement. He decided just what leader would be best fitted to lead each colony and what sort of workers each village would need.

Then, on Sunday, when all of the Saints had gathered for worship, at first under the interlaced branches and willows of the bowery and later in the adobe tabernacle, he would stand at the pulpit and describe a new place chosen for settlement. The new village would need a miller, a blacksmith, a shoemaker, a midwife, a school teacher. It would need many good farmers and builders.

The people moved uneasily, wondering if Brother Brigham would "read out" their names to go to some faraway place. If a man's name was "read out" he might have a week or a month to get everything in order to leave his home and his business. He was usually expected to take his entire family with him, including his married sons and their families. Brigham Young was counting on the young people to help just as he was counting on their fathers and mothers. There was work for everybody in the new land.

Sometimes Brigham Young did not read out the names. Sometimes he described the new place and then called for volunteers. And sometimes when a man he needed for an important project did not live in Salt Lake Valley he wrote a letter.

Here is a letter that was sent to a young father in the little mountain town of Coalville.

>President's Office
>Great Salt Lake City
>April 12, 1867

Elder Ira Hinckley
Dear Brother:

We wish to get a good and suitable person to settle on and take charge of the Church Ranch at Cove Creek, Millard County. Your name has been suggested for this position. As it is some distance from any other settlement, a man of sound, practical judgment and experience is needed to fill the place. Cove Creek is on the main road to Dixie and Lower California, some forty-two miles south of Fillmore and some twenty miles north of Beaver.

If you think you can take this mission you should endeavor to go south with us. We expect to start a week from Monday. It is not wisdom for you to take your family there until after a fort is built. There is a mail and telegraph station there. Should you conclude to go let me know by the bearer of this letter and when you start come prepared with conveyance to accompany us.

>*Your brother in the gospel,*
>*Brigham Young.*

P.S. The object of building a fort at Cove Creek is to offer protection from Indians to the telegraph and mail station and to travelers who are constantly on the road, also to furnish food and protection from the weather to this latter class. There is farming and hay land, also herding facilities, good firewood in abundance and close by.

>*B.Y.*

Although Ira Hinckley had only an hour to make up his mind and little more than a week to get ready for a new venture he, like most everyone else who heard Brigham Young's call, "concluded to go."

Although most of the men that Brigham Young called to make new homes would rather have stayed where they were, they were proud to have been chosen. They knew that only the best and strongest were called to do the difficult jobs. Besides, the people respected Brigham Young. They admired him, obeyed him, and loved him. To nearly all of them he was "Brother Brigham." And when he called them to a new "mission" they hurried to his office to say that they were ready to go.

Sometimes he called men who were unwilling to go. When they said that they did not want to go Brother Brigham reminded them that the Mormons believed in "free agency." That is, they believed that every man has a right to choose for himself. No man was forced to do anything against his will.

Brigham Young praised those who accepted the call, assigned them to a leader and told them where and when to have their supplies checked. Going to remote areas they would need to carry enough food to keep them until harvest. They would need farming tools and seed. They would need a supply of warm clothing and stout shoes. They would also need strong animals to pull their wagons, milk cows, sheep and chickens.

If they, themselves, could not supply these things, their neighbors often gave them a farewell party and brought with them a chicken, a quilt, a crock of lard, a new churn, or a bag of pumpkin seed.

What happened when the Mormons set out to colonize a new place?

One day George Albert Smith stood before the Saints in the tabernacle. He told them that Brigham Young had asked him to be in charge of the settlement of Southern Deseret (now called Utah.) He told about Little Salt Lake (now called Iron County). He didn't "read off" names but called for volunteers. One hundred and eighteen men, many of them young and without families, stood up and offered to go with him. These men waited to harvest their crops so they would have food to take with them. In December the one hundred and eighteen men with thirty families started south. They crossed five mountain ranges, driving oxen-drawn wagons and a few mule-drawn vehicles, herding their sheep and cattle before them. Finally on January the thirteenth they arrived at a place called Center Creek. The temperature was twelve degrees below zero. The women made the homes in the wagon boxes as comfortable as possible. The men and boys began to build a road into the canyon. Finally after five hundred work days—of course many men chalked up these hours, not just one man—they brought back a pole ninety-nine feet long. They erected the pole and raised the Stars and Stripes while the others stood and cheered. They fired a salute with the one cannon they had brought along. The cheers and the salute were for the Stars and Stripes whipping in the cold winds.

Even before they built homes they held an election and decided who the officers of the town should be and who should represent them in the General Assembly of Deseret. After election day a fort was built and all of the houses were built inside, with the fort's wall making the back wall of the houses. A church was built of hewn logs. The town was named Parowan. As soon as the necessary building was done, George Albert Smith turned his attention to a school. He was the teacher and he had thirty-five students in his class that first icy winter. The Mormon settlers were never too busy to build a church and a school. They believed that learning as much as they could about as many things as they could was a part of their religion.

Sometimes everything went well with the settlers. When they built new towns not too far from Salt Lake City they had to work very hard. Sometimes there was trouble with the Indians. But soon they had good homes and beautiful fields and orchards. Those who settled farther away from Salt Lake Valley had more adventures and more problems.

In June of 1849 the Ute Indian chief, Walkara, called *Walker* by the white people, came to Salt Lake City. He insisted on seeing Brigham Young. He wanted white men to come to Sanpitch Valley to teach the natives how to build homes and till the soil. Brigham Young sent an exploring party. They reached Chief Walkara's people in August and were received like kings.

In the early fall fifty families left Salt Lake City. They cleared roads and built bridges as they traveled south. Finally in late November they arrived at what is now Manti, Utah. The Indians received them warmly, but the welcome was the only thing that was warm. The weather was below freezing. At first the families lived in their wagon boxes but soon the snow began to drift higher and higher. The Indians showed them natural caves in the hillsides and the Mormons crawled into the caves like moles. Soon the women made the caves into comfortable homes—dark and small, but comfortable. It was not until spring came and the snakes who had been farther back in the caves began

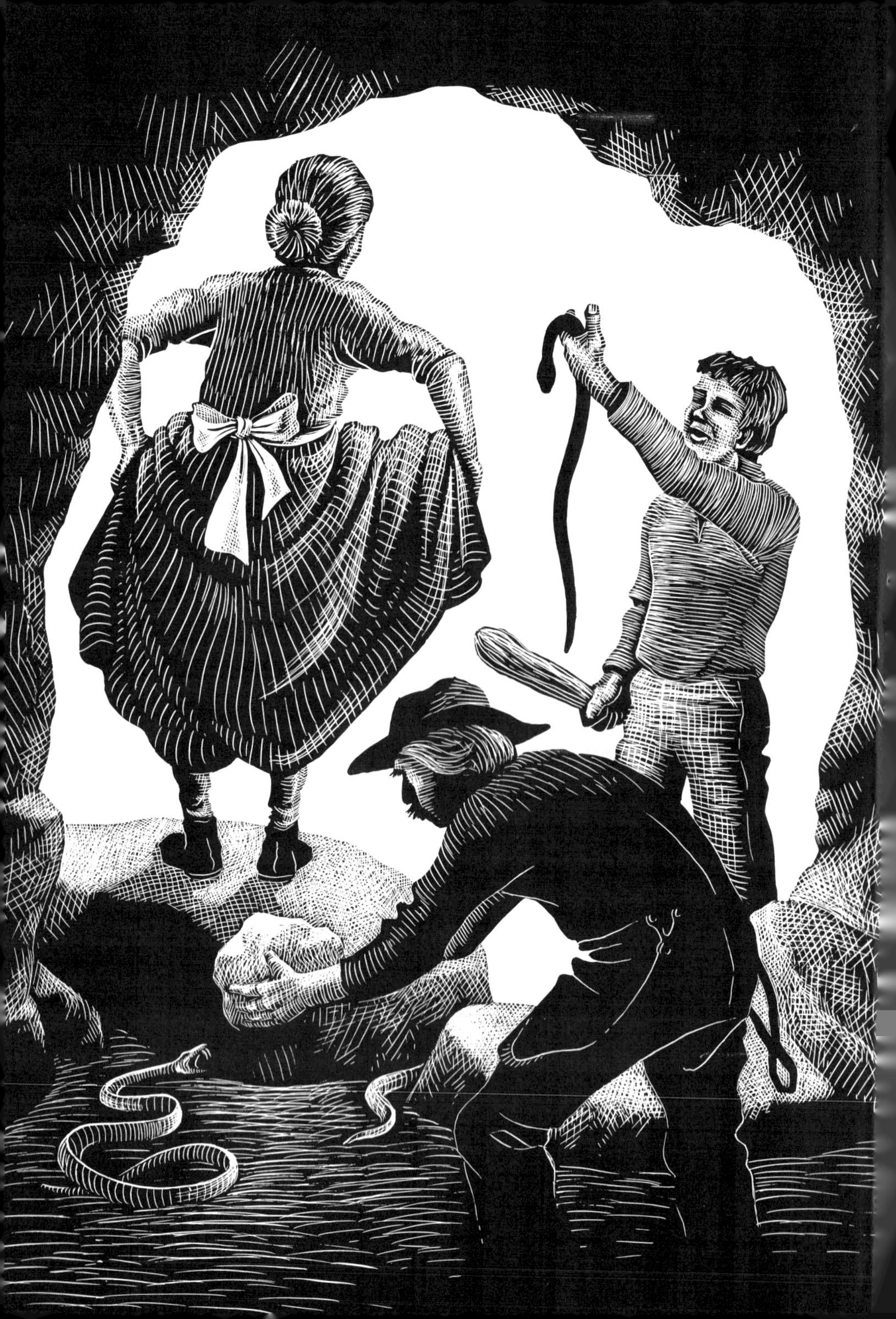

to waken from hibernation and seek the sunshine, that they discovered that all through the winter they had shared their apartments with rattlesnakes.

Far to the south of Salt Lake Valley Brother Brigham's scouts discovered a beautiful land that was so warm, even in the winter, that flowers bloomed outdoors. The Saints called this warm land Dixie. The low hills were a beautiful shade of red and the soil in the valley was so rich that sub-tropical crops of all kinds could be raised there.

In 1850 Brigham Young sent settlers to this valley. Their first work was to harness the Virgin River to irrigate the farm land. The Virgin River was just like a rebellious person. It would rest quietly while the Mormons built dams and ditches and canals. Then, when all of this work was done, it would go into flood, washing away the dams, breaking the banks of the canals, overrunning the ditches and washing out the fields.

Finally the people conquered the river and built a beautiful little city. Brigham Young built his winter home there.

In 1855 Brother Brigham sent a party—mostly men—to the Salmon River Valley three hundred and seventy-five miles north of Great Salt Lake. These men were to start a settlement; but their chief work was to teach the Indians.

Even reaching the headwaters of the Salmon River without so much as a trapper's trail to guide them, was hard. After twenty-two days of forced travel they did reach this beautiful place and began to build a fort called *Fort Lemhi*. At once they made friends with the Shoshone and Nez Perce Indians. They planted crops and began to teach the Indians. The first crop came up beautifully but it was eaten by the grasshoppers. Some of the men went back to Salt Lake Valley for more supplies. The second year the grasshoppers took the crops again. But the Mormons liked the Indians and the Indians liked the Mormons. One man wrote:

> *The Indians here are the noblest race I have seen in the West. They are very friendly. They say the white men are their friends. We are learning their language as fast as we can. . . .*

The colony grew. The soil was rich, the grasshoppers could be conquered and the fish seemed to jump out of the stream to meet the fishermen.

In 1857 the Saints gave a big feast for the Indians, but some of the Indians wouldn't eat. This was strange behavior! The next month the Indians began to be rude and they tried to steal horses and stock. Finally, in February, the Indians raided the settlement, drove off the stock, and shot at the Mormons. Three of the Saints were killed

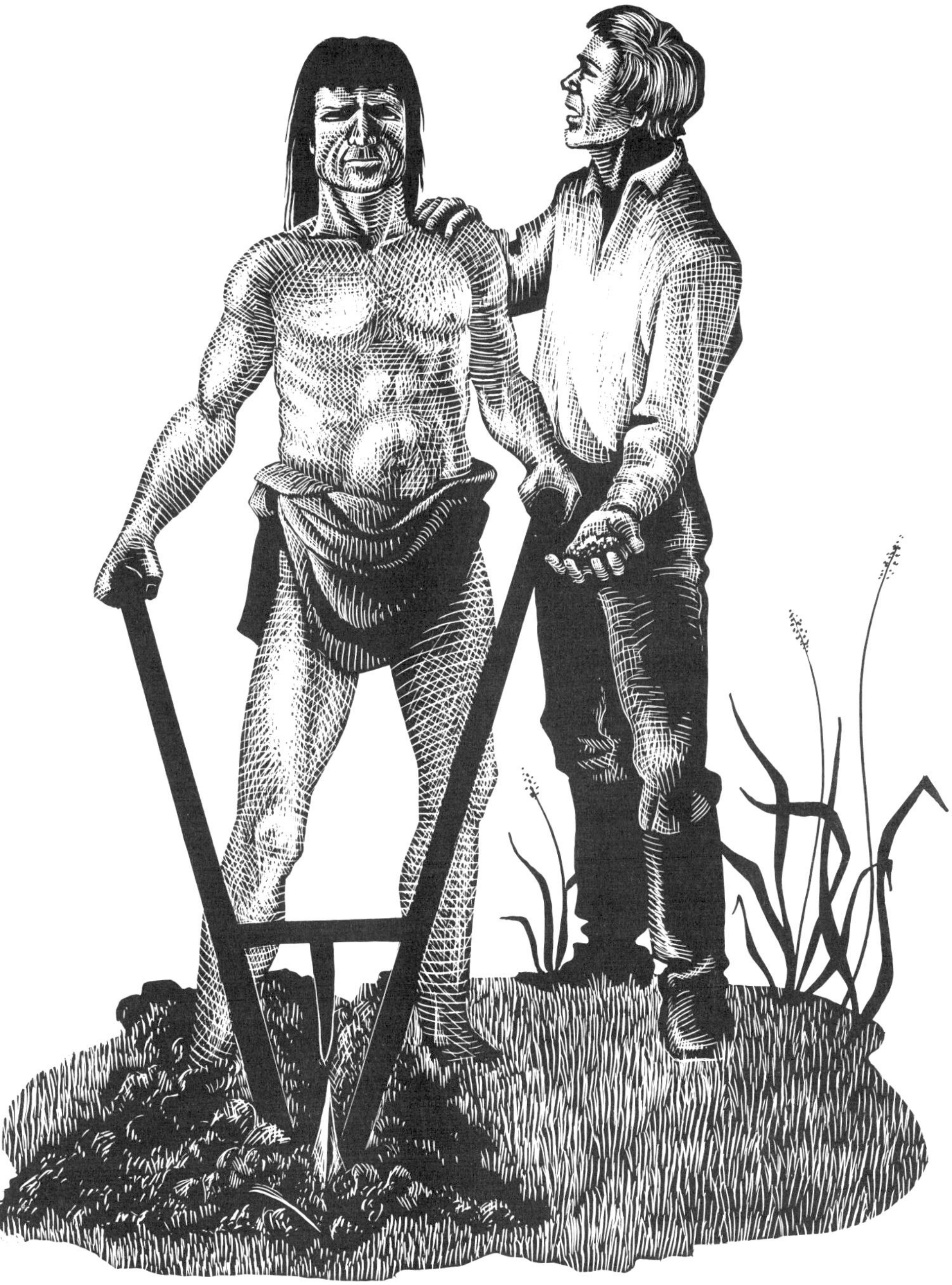

and seven were wounded. At last the reason for the change in the Indians was discovered. One of the men who had been left for dead, regained consciousness and crawled back to the fort after night closed in. He had seen a white man with the Indians. He even knew the white man's name. Later the Indians, themselves, said that they had been told that the Mormons were planning to "wipe out" the Indians.

When the settlers moved away from Fort Lemhi they gave much of their stock to the Indians. It was sixty years before Mormons returned to build homes in the Salmon River Valley.

But the Mormons who had the hardest time were those who took their families to the little oasis between the Virgin and Muddy Rivers in Nevada. These men and women didn't know about mosquitoes and malaria. They settled on the lowlands by the banks of the rivers. Everybody was sick. At times there weren't enough well people to care for the sick and bury the dead. They planted cotton and it grew and they harvested it. But they couldn't make shoes of cotton. They couldn't eat it. In the summer the weather was so hot that the barefooted boys ran along the dirt roads then lay down with their feet in the air to cool them. One lucky boy had a big hat. He put his hat on the ground and stood on it whenever his feet got too hot to endure.

The old folks died in the winter. The babies died in the summer. Everyone was hungry. They built excellent brick houses—some two-storied. They planted fields and laid out water systems. But when Brother Brigham visited them and saw how miserable they were tears came to his eyes. "This is more than anyone can endure," he said. So he gave up part of his dream and advised the Saints to move to a better place.

And so August 29, 1877, when the message went out over the telegraph wire: *Brigham Young is dead*, those who had worked so hard to help Brigham Young's sometimes impossible dream to come true, turned away sorrowing. There would never be another "Brother Brigham."

Brother Brigham was dead, but the Mormon Trail, built under his direction, stretched from Nauvoo to Salt Lake City. It did not end at Salt Lake City. It divided into several different strands. These strands had reached parts of Wyoming, Colorado, Idaho, Arizona, Nevada, New Mexico and California. Later they would reach into Old Mexico, and still later into Alberta, Canada.

And wherever the Trail went there was industry. There were quiet, peaceable farming communities where the people worked together, prayed together and played together. The Saints loved dancing and theatricals. They built opera houses and theaters. They organized orchestras and bands and choirs. They constructed schools and colleges and universities.

Changes have come to all of the Mormon settlements in the past hundred years. But the spirit of the pioneers that built the Mormon Trail has been passed along to their children, their grandchildren and their great-grandchildren. This spirit is called the *Mormon Heritage*.

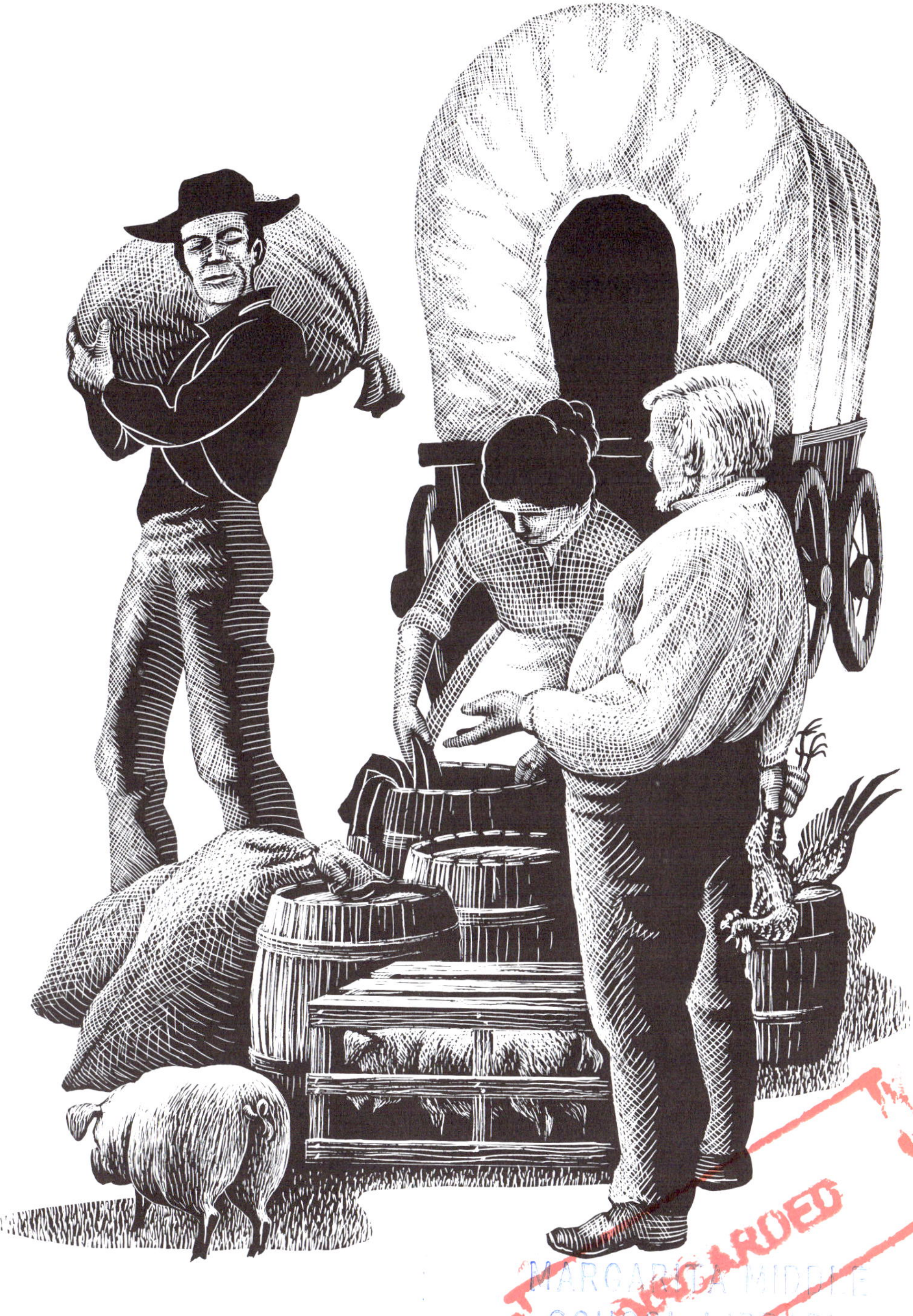